ANTHROPOLOGICAL PAPERS

MUSEUM OF ANTHROPOLOGY, UNIVERSITY OF MICHIGAN
NO. 42

THE OCCUPATIONS OF MIGRANTS IN GHANA

BY
POLLY HILL
Fellow, Clare Hall, Cambridge

ANN ARBOR
THE UNIVERSITY OF MICHIGAN, 1970

ACKNOWLEDGEMENTS

I wish to express my gratitude to the Center for Research on Economic Development, The University of Michigan, Ann Arbor, for so generously supporting my research from 1965 to 1969 and for providing a portion of the funds for this publication. I am, also, most grateful to Mr. Ivor Wilks for criticising some of the entries in Part II of this paper—it being hardly necessary to add that I alone am responsible for the numerous judgments and estimates there presented.

Polly Hill
October, 1969

CONTENTS

Introduction		1
Part I:	Migrant Populations	5
	Section 1. The "Migratory Ethnic Groups"	5
	Section 2. A Classification of Ethnic Groups in terms of the Occupations of Migrant Men	9
	Section 3. The Geographical Distribution of the Migrant Population	23
	Section 4. Urbanization	25
	Section 5. Summary of Preceding Statistics	28
	Section 6. The Sex Ratios of the Migrant Populations	31
	Section 7. The Occupations of Migrant Women	33
Part II:	Notes on each of the 34 "Migratory Ethnic Groups"	35
	Southern Ghanaian Ethnic Groups	36
	Northern and Non-Ghanaian Ethnic Groups	40
Appendix I.	Notes on the Census Concept of "Tribe"	57
Appendix II.	Demographic Anthropology: Migration on Marriage	61
Appendix III.	The "Foreign Origin" Population	63
Appendix IV.	The Census Concept of "Locality"	65
Appendix V.	Notes on Occupational Classification in the Census	67
Appendix VI.	Estimates of the total numbers of Cocoa Farmers, *Abusa* Labourers and other Cocoa-Farm Labourers	73
References		75

TABLES

1.	The "Migratory Ethnic Groups": Total Population in Ghana	7
2.	Occupations of Males Fifteen Years and Over (Numbers)	14
3.	Occupations of Males Fifteen Years and Over (Percentages)	19
4.	Migrants in Six Northern Ghanaian Ethnic Groups	21
5.	Degree of Urbanization: Southern Ghanaian "Migratory Ethnic Groups"	26

6A. Degree of Urbanization: Northern and Non-Ghanaian "Migratory Ethnic Groups" 27

6B. Degree of Urbanization: Six Northern Ghanaian Ethic Groups ... 28

7. Occupation and Geographical Distribution of Migrants 29

8. The Sex Ratios of Northern Ghanaian Ethnic Groups 32

9. The Sex Ratios of Non-Ghanaian Ethnic Groups 32

10. Female Occupations 34

INTRODUCTION

The scope of this statistical study on the occupations of migrants in Ghana is very limited: statistically based on the 1960 Ghana population census, it is primarily an attempt to show that "economically motivated migration" takes a much greater variety of occupational forms than is conventionally, or commonly, supposed. Although the analysis is conducted in terms of ethnic group, this does not reflect any belief in the immutability of ethnic occupational preferences, which are constantly undergoing change. Occupational statistics are cross-analysed in the census reports in a number of ways, and it happens that the analysis by ethnic group is much more illuminating for present purposes than, for instance, the analysis by local authority area. Besides, "ethnic occupational specialization" still remains a most striking phenomenon.

Economists naturally refer to the migration of *labour* (without qualification): but this tends to imply both that most "economically motivated migration" in West Africa involves employment (proper) in mines, factories, government service and so forth (as it does in many other African as well as non-African, parts of the world), and that migration involves increased urbanization. It is a primary purpose of this analysis to emphasize that many migrants work as farmers and in other non-wage-earning occupations and that many are attracted to the countryside, not only as labourers and farmers, but also as traders.

The astonishing Yoruba are a case in point. These Nigerian migrants, both men and women, are spread evenly over the whole of Ghana; they are found in every one of the 69 local authority areas (which existed in 1960) to the degree that a Ghanaian marketplace might almost be defined as a concourse of buyers and sellers such that at least two or three of the sellers are Yoruba women. As for Yoruba men, they percolate deeply into the countryside, tapping a great variety of neglected economic opportunities. They tend to operate behind the scenes as collectors and processors of produce; they have a strong aversion to the limitations imposed by wage-earning employment. There is, as yet, no literature on this migration; but this analysis does at least draw attention to the astonishing fact that the detailed geographical distribution of the Yoruba population in Ghana closely resembles that of the entire population.

A secondary purpose of this article is to provide reference

material (see Part II) relating to the 34 "migratory ethnic groups" which were selected from the census list as representative of migrants in Ghana.

Finally, a few relevant census concepts, such as those relating to "locality" and "foreign origin population," receive brief critical examination.

Although the art of census-taking was developed in "advanced" countries and although the Ghana census-takers sought to conform, so far as reasonably possible, to certain international classifications, the various reports on the 1960 Ghana Census, which are greatly superior to those for any other West African country, show what intelligent flexibility in census-planning can achieve, even though the population is so ethnically heterogenous as to provide us with laboratory conditions for studying migration.

I had originally hoped that some kind of "typology of migration" might emerge from this analysis—that it might assist in the definition of some of the basic terms which we all employ so light-heartedly when studying that complex phenomenon "migration." I now think that this was to put the cart before the horse. The *Shorter Oxford Dictionary* defines demography as "that branch of anthropology (*sic*) which treats of the statistics of births, deaths, diseases, etc.," and West African demographers have not made the additional subject of "migration" one of their specialities; until much more systematic fieldwork has been undertaken by anthropologists, economists and sociologists, I think that they would be wise not to do so, owing to the danger of the hardening of such current myths on migration as would be bound to bias their whole approach.

Therefore, I am here attempting to make the best of an intellectually unsatisfying situation. Were I to have called the census definitions in question at all radically, I should have been denying the possibility that the statistics on which they had been based had any useful content. To make this quite clear I have simply taken the census statistics as given, and tried to extract what I can from them. It would have been pointless to have attempted any formal definitions of such basic concepts as "migrant" or "homeland" beyond what is implied by saying that a migrant is one who resides (and probably works) outside the geographical homeland of his ethnic group. One must accept that much of the analysis is necessarily timeless: the census analyses are such that one must regard all Hausa as migrants, even though one knows (as some Tables of the census report confirm) that many of them were born in Ghana. Even so, I hope that the statistics may be regarded as useful background material for those fieldworkers who seek to widen our knowledge of "migration"—thus, incidentally, making the collection of better census statistics ultimately possible.

INTRODUCTION

This monograph was first written in 1966, soon after the publication of the census volume *Tribes in Ghana*. Since then *The Population of Tropical Africa* edited by J. C. Caldwell and C. Okonjo (1968) has appeared, being a record of the first African population conference held at the University of Ibadan in January, 1966. This useful, long, practical, authoritative and well-edited volume contains no significant discussion of census definitions of "tribe," occupation and "locality"–thus strengthening my belief that non-demographers serve a useful purpose in offering well-intentioned critical analyses of statistics based on those concepts in this branch of anthropology.

Since this monograph was written the migrant community in Ghana has been radically affected by the Alien Deportation Order of 1969, which has resulted in the departure of hundreds of thousands of non-Ghanaian West Africans. It is thought that this study may have added value as an analysis of the composition of the migrant community prior to this enactment. Unfortunately the most recent census, that of 1970 (the results of which are in any case not yet available), will show only the initial effects on the alien community of the Order.

I
MIGRANT POPULATIONS

SECTION 1

THE "MIGRATORY ETHNIC GROUPS"

As many as 92 "tribes,"[1] here referred to as ethnic groups, were separately distinguished[2] in the 1960 Ghana population census, the "tribal" statistics all being presented in *Special Report "E": Tribes in Ghana* (Gil et al., 1964). Statistical tables with 92 entries are cumbersome, and for this and other reasons it was decided to base this analysis on a selection of ethnic groups whose men have a marked propensity to migrate.

In compiling this list a start was made by including any ethnic group such that a substantial proportion of its members had been born outside Ghana. There were 21 of these groups, 19 of which were (somewhat arbitrarily in a few cases) regarded as non-Ghanaian,[3] in the sense that no significant proportion of them was recorded[4] as settled in Ghana in a district (or districts) which, perhaps as a result of earlier[5] migrations, might appropriately be regarded as part of the homeland. The remaining two groups were the Ewe and the Busanga, both of them frontier-straddling.

---

[1] See Appendix I on the census concept of "tribe". Although the term "ethnic group" is used here in place of the old-fashioned "tribe" employed in the census, it must be re-emphasized that many of the census groupings cannot be regarded as "ethnic" according to any rigorous understanding of that word. Sometimes they are merely inhabitants of a particular town or locality (See also Part II).

[2] In some tables in the census volume *Tribes in Ghana* some tribes are combined into larger groups: incredibly enough, the Yoruba and the Ibo are sometimes grouped.

[3] This is without regard to the question of the proportion of individuals who were counted as of "foreign origin" for census purposes (see Appendix III). The "Non-Ghanaian" ethnic groups are all those included under the heading "Northern Ghanaians and Non-Ghanaians" in Table 1, except for the 7 Northern Ghanaian groups which are numbers 11, 12, 13, 15, 21, 24 and 30.

[4] All the statistics in *Tribes in Ghana* were blown up on the basis of a 10 percent sample of the full census data, and are therefore subject to sampling variability. Readers are asked to bear this in mind as well as to note that, for the sake of convenience, qualifications such as "estimated", "recorded" . . . , which should strictly be attached to all cited figures, have been omitted. I am well aware that the sampling error attached to many of the smaller figures is so great that it is questionable whether they should be quoted at all; the same doubt attaching, in many instances, to their original publication. However, rather than devoting a great deal of labour to considering which figures it is justifiable to quote and which should be rejected (and the confidence limits attached to the former), I have decided to go ahead as though the sample figures (which, of course, all end in zero) were a full count. Professional statisticians are asked to use their own discretion in interpreting the figures (after reference, if need be, to *Tribes in Ghana*, specially to sections 5.1 and 5.2 which deal with sample design and sampling variability) and to appreciate the difficulties encountered by a research worker equipped only with a slide rule.

[5] This loose use of terms results from the necessary timelessness of our practical definition of a migrant.

Of other Ghanaian ethnic groups, all those were included for which a high proportion of persons had been enumerated in a region[6] other than the one in which they were born. As for intra-regional migration, a glance at the census table[7] showing the distribution of the population between the 69 local authority areas, as defined in 1960, was often sufficient to reveal the existence of longer distance intra-regional migration. There were, however, a few interesting migratory groups, such as the Konkomba, who were included because the literature records them as migratory, although they happened to slip through this statistical net. Finally, some attempt was made to include some migratory peoples with a notably low capacity to become assimilated,[8] although a high proportion of those living outside their homeland had been born in the area where they were enumerated. Including the Ewe and the Busanga, there were altogether 15 Ghanaian migratory groups, of which 7 were classified as Northern Ghanaian.

No use was made of the statistics in the census report relating to those born in a *locality* other than that in which they were enumerated. Considering all the difficulties involved in defining locality (see Appendix IV, p.63 for census definition) and the fact that strict application of the definition would often result in designating nearly everyone who "moves house" in certain areas of dispersed settlement as "migrant,"[9] this material seems valueless for our purposes.[10]

The total number of persons recorded as belonging to the 34 "migratory ethnic groups" which were so selected, comprised over 40 percent of the whole population of Ghana.[11] As Table 1 shows, the groups varied greatly in size, ranging from 873,000 Ewe and 202,000 Dagarti at the one extreme, to 1,030 Bawle and 5,100 Songhai (Gao) at the other.

The Notes in Part II on each of these 34 "migratory ethnic groups" include some criticisms of the tribal definitions used in the census[12] and I know that others, many of them far better qualified

---

[6]At that time Ghana was divided into six regions - Western, Eastern, Volta, Ashanti, Brong-Ahafo and Northern. For census purposes the Accra Capital District, which included Tema and the Ga-Dangbe-Shai local council area, was carved out of the Eastern region and regarded as a seventh region.

[7]Table S1 of *Tribes in Ghana*.

[8]For instance, certain migrant cocoa farmers of southern Ghana.

[9]In Birmingham *et al.*, 1966, Table 6.7 (p.132), a "short-distance migrant" is defined as one enumerated outside the locality in which he was born, but in the same region. Apart from the objection to regarding one who "moves house" as a migrant, many of the 7 regions were so large that much intra-regional migration was "long distance".

[10]See Appendix II for the suggestion that valid use may be made of this material in providing rough relative indicators of the propensity of women of different ethnic groups to migrate short distances on marriage.

[11]No attempt is made here to estimate the proportion of the total population of the 34 ethnic groups which might be held to be "migrant".

[12]The "Ethnological Synopsis of the Major Tribes in Ghana," included in *Tribes in Ghana*, is rather unreliable, and presents much casual, pseudo-anthropological material of doubtful relevance.

TABLE 1

THE "MIGRATORY ETHNIC GROUPS":
TOTAL POPULATION IN GHANA

Ethnic Group	Population	Percentage of Males Born Abroad	Sex Ratio*
Southern Ghanaians			
1. "Akwapim"	144,790	—	100
2. Anum-Boso	18,340	—	93
3. Ewe	872,860	13†	100
4. Krobo	162,940	—	96
5. Kwahu	131,970	—	92
6. Kyerepon	33,780	—	86
7. Larteh	22,330	—	91
8. Shai	20,970	—	99
Northern Ghanaians and Non-Ghanaians			
9. Atakpame	8,530	77	125
10. Bawle	1,030	61	171
11. Builsa	62,620	—	101
12. Busanga	56,690	28	130
13. Dagarti	201,680	6	104
14. Fon	3,370	81	179
15. Frafra	138,370	1	106
16. Fulani	25,050	61	202
17. Grusi, n.e.s.	41,180	23	164
18. Gurma, n.e.s.	21,850	42	308
19. Hausa	61,730	56	163
20. Ibo	14,050	80	161
21. Konkomba	110,150	5	102
22. Kotokoli	51,020	47	97
23. Kru	6,500	80	169
24. Kusasi	121,610	1	108
25. "Kyamba"	48,720	36	102
26. Lobi	37,550	45	112
27. Mossi	106,140	72	284
28. Pilapila	24,790	46	105
29. Songhai (Gao)	5,100	94	827
30. Wala	47,200	1	105
31. "Wangara"	34,180	50	129
32. Yoruba	100,560	62	116
33. Zabrama	30,830	87	506
34. "Other Nigerians"	24,350	71	110

*Number of males per 100 females.
†It is thought that this percentage is far too low, many Ewe from Togo having stated that Ghana was their birthplace.

than myself in this field, are much more critical. Some of these critics, indeed, regard the census tribal classifications as virtually worthless and deplore any attempt, such as I am making here, to put the statistics so classified to any practical use. I am obliged to take the census classification as given, well aware though I am that, for instance, many terms, such as "Grusi," may refer to no specific ethnic group— in that particular case the term being merely an "objective classifier" for a certain group of languages—that many "tribes" lack ethnic homogeneity, and so forth.

Despite the critics, whose feelings I understand and partly share, I am encouraged in this task by the internal consistency of much of the material relating to occupations, which suggests that the census-takers did a better job than might have been expected considering that enumerators were merely instructed (see Appendix I) to obtain (from all African informants) "what their tribe is and write it down in the space provided." Even in some of those cases where much doubt is thrown on the appropriateness of the tribal name adopted in the census, it yet seemed that so far as migrants were concerned the group might have a distinct identity, justifying its separate treatment.

One reason for including as many as 34 ethnic groups in the somewhat arbitrarily compiled list, was the wish to throw up as many different "types" of migration as possible. If the small groups of Atakpame and Fon had been excluded there would have been no instances of extreme specialization of migrants on a single craft, in these cases building work.

On the other hand, our statistical analysis of the occupations of migrants presents a picture which is far from complete. Thus, there are some important ethnic groups which are excluded from the list although certain sections of them have a high propensity to migrate, two examples being the Ashanti (sections of whom are very apt to migrate as cocoa farmers) and the Fanti who often migrate as fishermen or as farmers, or in search of "professional-clerical" and other employment (proper). Then there were some distinct, though small, ethnic groups which could not be included in our list owing to the insistence of migrants on designating themselves as members of larger, better-known, groups; an example being the Tallensi of northeastern Ghana, who speak of themselves as Frafra when away from home.

SECTION 2

A CLASSIFICATION OF ETHNIC GROUPS IN TERMS OF THE OCCUPATIONS OF MIGRANT MEN

The idea behind this classification of the 34 ethnic groups in terms of the occupations of migrant men, is that there are great variations between groups in the extent to which migrants work in the following five main classes of occupation, namely farming, farm-labouring, other types of employment (proper), trading, and other "own account" occupations.

The main census statistics on which this classification is based are here presented in Tables 2, 3 and 4.

The number of each ethnic group is recorded after its name in order to facilitate reference to the Notes on Ethnic Groups in Part II of this paper, which contains much material not repeated here.

Class (i): The Migrant Food-farmers
(Men, and Their Families, Mainly Migrate As Food-farmers)

      Krobo   (4)
      Konkomba (21)
      Lobi   (26)

The Konkomba and Lobi are "seeping migrants," whose movement is (presumably) mainly motivated by the search for better farming land; they are apt to be constantly on the move in the sense that they do not intend to settle permanently in one place, and are involved in a one-way process, there being no thought of returning to the "homeland"; whole compounds remove or segments hive off. The Krobo migrants, by contrast, buy chronological "sequences" of land in the uplands, intending to abandon none of their earlier acquisitions; they remain sociologically linked with their homeland in the plain.

Class (ii): The Migrant Cocoa-farmers
(High proportions of the male migrant populations are cocoa-farmers who, themselves or their forebears, had purchased chronological "sequences" of land)

      "Akwapim" (1)
      Anum-Bosò (2)
      Kyerepon (6)
      Larteh   (7)
      Shai   (8)

All the principal migratory cocoa-farmers of Southern Ghana

are included in this list, with the exception of the Krobo who more often migrate as food-farmers—see (i) above. This migration, which began about 1890, will not be described here, being fully dealt with in Hill, 1963.

The recorded percentages of occupied males who are cocoa-farmers are: Shai (47%), Anum-Boso (42%), Kyerepon (40%), "Akwapim" and Larteh (each 39%). Nearly all cocoa-farmers are migrants.

Class (iii): The Specialist Migrant Farm-labourers
(High proportions—49 percent or more, of occupied males are farm-labourers, mainly on cocoa-farms, the proportions in "other employment" being in all cases less than half that in farming)

        Gurma, n.e.s. (18)
        Kusasi (24)
        "Kyamba" (25)
        Mossi (27)
        Pilapila (28)

In the cases of the Gurma (70%), Pilapila (62%), Mossi (52%) and "Kyamba" (49%), about half, or more, of all occupied males are farm-labourers; if the 8 percent of Gurma who were recorded as food-farmers represent the non-migrant population, then about 76 percent of all occupied Gurma migrants are farm-labourers, mainly cocoa-labourers. As for the Kusasi, it appears from the estimates in Table 4 that about 75 percent of migrant males are farm-labourers, most of them probably in cocoa.

The "Kyamba" also migrate to a significant extent as food-farmers (26% of all occupied males); they percolate through to neighbouring Buem-Krakye (in Ghana) from their homeland in Togo.

Class (iv): The General Urban and Rural Proletariat, Exclusive of Those Whose Members Work as Miners to Any Significant Extent
(In all cases: (*a*) the proportion of occupied males who are employed as farm-labourers is lower than for the ethnic groups, in class (iii); and (*b*) the proportion in non-farming employment is at least half that in farming employment)

        Builsa (11)
        Busanga (12)
        Fulani (16)
        Grusi, n.e.s (17)
        Kotokoli (22)
        "Wangara" (31)

For the Grusi, the Kotokoli and the "Wangara," the proportions of all occupied males employed in farming and non-farming work were respectively, 38 and 37, 37 and 20, and 38 and 27 percent.

It is estimated (see Table 4) that about 22 percent of all Builsa occupied males are migrants; of these about 65 percent are in non-farm employment, about 25 percent in farm employment.

With the Busanga it is estimated that about 58 percent of all occupied males are migrant; of these about 51 percent are in non-farm employment, about 42 percent in farm employment. The rather arbitrary definition of "migrant" however, should be noted in this instance.

Although 21 percent of occupied Fulani males were recorded as engaged in work with livestock, this ethnic group has been included in this class, as farm employment (20%) and non-farm employment (23%) were equally important occupations.

Class (v): The General Urban and Rural Proletariat, Inclusive of Those Whose Members Work to a Significant Extent as Miners

(As class (iv) inclusive of those who are apt to work as miners)

> Dagarti (13)
> Frafra (15)
> Wala (30)

It is estimated (see Table 4) that the percentages of all occupied migrants who are in farming, mining, and other non-farming employment are:

Group	Farming	Mining	Other
Dagarti (13)	46	13	36
Frafra (15)	29	13	51
Wala (30)	17	15	37

Class (vi): Traders and "Own Account" Workers with a Marked Reluctance to Work In Employment (Proper) of Any Type

Yoruba (32)

Nearly half (48%) of all Yoruba occupied males are in trading and a further 20 percent are in other "own account" work. Only 15 percent of occupied males are in non-farming employment and only 4 percent are farm workers.

Class (vii): Men with a Marked Willingness to Work in Many Types of Non-Farming Employment, but Who Have A Strong Aversion to Farming-Employment

Ibo (20)

Over half (52%) of all occupied Ibo males are in non-farming employment, a higher proportion than for any other "migratory ethnic group." (Only 3% of occupied Ibo males are farm-workers.)

Class (viii): Men Who Are Mainly Traders, "Own Account" Workers and Non-Farming Employees, Again With A Strong Aversion to Farming-Employment

Hausa (19)
Songhai (Gao) (29)
"Other Nigerians" (34)

PERCENTAGE OCCUPIED MALES

Group	Non-farming employment	Farming employment	Trading	Other "Own" Account"
Hausa (19)	27	4	31*	18
Songhai (Gao) (29)	44	7	34	10
"Other Nigerians" (34)	34	4	20	19

*Includes butchers.

Class (ix): Men Who Are Predominantly Traders and Other "Own Account" Workers, But Who Are Also Prepared to Take Employment in Both Farming and Non-Farming Occupations

Zabrama (33)

Nearly half of all Zabrama occupied males (48%) are "own account" workers of whom 28% are traders; although only 14 percent of Zabrama were recorded as in farming employment, a further 10 percent were recorded as being "farmers," probably mainly labourers who had evolved into farmers.

Class (x): Occupational Specialists (Building-Workers and Seamen)

Atakpame (9)
Fon (14)
Kru (25)

Building-workers comprise about 53 percent of all occupied

male Atakpame, the corresponding figure for the Fon being 39 percent; the remaining Atakpame are mainly farm-workers, the remaining Fon are mainly in rural or urban employment.

Although the Kru are well-known as specialist seamen, it seems that no more than half (at the most) of occupied males are so employed, and the proportion may be far lower. Other types of employment (proper) account for most of the remainder.

Class (xi): Miscellaneous Unclassifiable

    Ewe (3)
    Kwahu (5)
    Bawle (10)

The occupational statistics relating to the Ewe are hard to interpret for present purposes, as migrants and non-migrants cannot be distinguished. All that can be stated is that the Ewe are apt to migrate in the following capacities among others: cocoa-farmers, cocoa-labourers, general-labourers, specialist employees (such as fitters, sawyers, and "services"), professional/clerical, food-farmers, fishermen (sea and river) and other workers on "own account."

The Kwahu are pre-eminently engaged in cocoa-farming - 45 percent of all occupied males being farmers or *abusa* labourers (mainly the former). There being little information on the extent to which Kwahu cocoa-farmers are migrant, this ethnic group is here left unclassified.

THE OCCUPATIONS OF MIGRANTS IN GHANA

TABLE

OCCUPATIONS OF MALES

(In

Ethnic Group	Food Farmers (1)	Cocoa Farmers or *Abusa* Labourers (2)	Farm Labourers (other) (3)	General Labourers (4)	Mine Labourers (5)	"Service" Occupations (6)
Southern Ghanaians						
1. "Akwapim"	3,690	12,210	1,690	750	(. .)	610
2. Anum-Boso	370	1,460	150	(. .)	—	(. .)
3. Ewe	51,400	28,180	9,590	5,690	400	5,910
4. Krobo	15,590	10,060	980	410	(. .)	370
5. Kwahu	1,350	11,090	740	370	(. .)	330
6. Kyerepon	1,540	2,750	480	(. .)	(. .)	(. .)
7. Larteh	590	1,730	170	(. .)	—	(. .)
8. Shai	750	2,130	330	(. .)	—	(. .)
Northern Ghanaians and Non-Ghanaians						
9. Atakpame	(. .)	590	390	(. .)	(. .)	—
10. Bawle	(. .)	130	(. .)	(. .)	—	(. .)
11. Builsa	13,020	150	850	1,650	(. .)	850
12. Busanga	6,910	1,280	3,140	3,740	330	1,110
13. Dagarti	31,680	1,430	6,060	5,200	2,060	930
14. Fon	100	110	170	170	(. .)	(. .)
15. Frafra	22,660	570	4,060	5,650	1,240	1,920
16. Fulani	1,470	420	1,810	1,150	130	780
17. Grusi, n.e.s.	2,280	1,700	4,560	3,610	380	1,640
18. Gurma, n.e.s.	1,050	2,480	8,710	970	190	500
19. Hausa	1,970	160	800	2,550	600	1,620
20. Ibo	170	120	(. .)	580	430	780
21. Konkomba	26,000	200	640	230	—	(. .)
22. Kotokoli	2,270	1,820	4,330	1,500	140	350
23. Kru	120	(. .)	(. .)	1,200	100	380
24. Kusasi	25,600	1,850	3,970	1,390	(. .)	420
25. "Kyamba"	3,060	2,880	2,850	940	(. .)	240
26. Lobi	8,440	780	1,160	130	(. .)	(. .)
27. Mossi	8,970	7,240	21,830	6,030	950	2,460
28. Pilapila	590	1,960	3,860	370	110	160
29. Songhai (Gao)	110	(. .)	180	410	130	440
30. Wala	7,760	170	350	900	440	210
31. "Wangara"	1,300	2,610	1,340	1,410	330	730
32. Yoruba	1,310	430	560	910	1,260	990
33. Zabrama	2,100	660	2,390	3,190	1,080	1,260
34. "Other Nigerians"	380	150	100	630	180	1,280

Notes:—(. .) Signifies figures between 10 and 90 inclusive, the actual figures are not given, as they convey a spurious sense of accuracy.

(i) The *source* of the statistics is Table S 26 in *Tribes in Ghana*. All the figures are based on a 10 percent sample, see footnote 5.

MIGRANT POPULATIONS

2

FIFTEEN YEARS AND OLDER
Numbers)

Other Employment (7)	Professional/Clerical (8)	Traders (9)	Diamond Diggers (10)	Drivers (11)	Tailors (12)	Carpenters (13)	Other "Own Account" (14)	Total Occupied (15)
1,130	4,750	1,020	(. .)	1,640	500	770	1,480	31,270
100	360	110	—	150	(. .)	140	290	3,480
6,710	13,120	4,010	260	4,330	4,780	12,570	21,060	194,120
940	1,790	650	(. .)	730	410	1,150	1,700	37,390
750	2,850	2,240	(. .)	1,390	1,340	170	740	24,860
200	520	140	—	250	(. .)	240	320	6,850
160	550	180	—	230	(. .)	190	400	4,430
190	220	(. .)	—	170	(. .)	230	220	4,550
(. .)	110	—	(. .)	(. .)	(. .)	—	1,540	2,930
(. .)	(. .)	(. .)	—	—	(. .)	(. .)	—	440
160	190	(. .)	(. .)	(. .)	(. .)	(. .)	(. .)	17,560
310	(. .)	390	180	(. .)	(. .)	(. .)	170	18,230
440	670	(. .)	410	100	130	(. .)	(. .)	50,810
(. .)	(. .)	(. .)	(. .)	. . .	(. .)	(. .)	510	1,480
770	290	850	430	(. .)	(. .)	150	280	40,060
570	260	820	240	130	380	(. .)	120	11,340
410	170	390	(. .)	210	150	(. .)	230	16,670
230	(. .)	160	(. .)	110	(. .)	(. .)	(. .)	12,370
1,330	920	5,100	1,540	750	1,460	(. .)	740	24,380
1,220	320	1,040	140	180	(. .)	(. .)	270	5,580
(. .)	(. .)	(. .)	—	(. .)	(. .)	(. .)	(. .)	27,400
310	100	1,180	120	470	320	(. .)	180	11,640
330	(. .)	(. .)	—	(. .)	—	(. .)	(. .)	2,780
210	170	130	(. .)	(. .)	(. .)	(. .)	(. .)	34,270
150	130	320	(. .)	160	230	100	260	11,610
(. .)	(. .)	(. .)	—	(. .)	—	(. .)	(. .)	10,780
2,420	580	1,760	370	460	440	(. .)	360	56,110
(. .)	140	430	(. .)	(. .)	130	(. .)	150	6,270
650	(. .)	1,250	200	(. .)	(. .)	. . .	(. .)	3,690
230	260	360	(. .)	150	330	(. .)	180	11,870
370	260	570	(. .)	230	320	(. .)	350	10,540
(. .)	1,440	13,360	1,600	710	1,890	240	1,190	28,080
950	230	5,830	2,180	(. .)	350	(. .)	150	21,170
360	470	1,410	710	130	190	(. .)	320	7,140

(ii) All the statistics relate, of course, to the total male population (aged 15 and over) and not to migrants. (Estimated figures relating to migrants only are given in Table 4 for six Northern Ghanaian ethnic groups.)

(iii) See Appendix V (Notes on Occupational Classification).

(continued on next page)

16 THE OCCUPATIONS OF MIGRANTS IN GHANA

TABLE 2 (Footnotes continued)

Explanation of Column Headings

(2) See Appendix V for an explanation as to why *abusa* labourers are included with cocoa farmers—an *abusa* labourer being a man who is employed by a cocoa farmer, being rewarded with a one-third share of the crop. See, also, the Notes on columns (2) and (3) of Table 3.

(3) All farm-labourers, other than *abusa* labourers, are included here.

(4) The term "general labourers" is used to denote the residuary census group "labourers, not elsewhere specified"; it basically covers all unskilled workers as well as such craft-workers as are not included in columns (11), (12), (13) (see below); it includes both light and heavy physical work: presumably most building-workers fall into this category.

(5) and (10) Mine labourers employed by mining companies are in column (5); the diamond diggers in column (10) work on their own account, being popularly known as "African diamond winners."

(6) The "service" occupations include policemen, domestic workers, caretakers of buildings, barbers, photographers and port workers (excluding longshoremen).

(7) See Appendix V with regard to the definition of employment. The main types of employment included here are loggers, "toolmakers . . . and related workers" (probably mainly fitters), electricians, longshoremen and freight handlers (including drivers' mates).

(8) Nurses, doctors, teachers, civil servants, business men, members of the armed forces, all types of professional people, clergy, typists, postal agents, letter-writers and even the so-called "fetish priests" are included under the heading "professional/clerical." Policemen are classified under "services," col (6).

(9) The census category "sales workers" is here denoted as "traders." Perhaps anyone who works mainly in a market, such as a market porter, is included here, though, for all one knows, such people might rather have been classed as "general labourers," column (4).

(11), (12) and (13) Drivers, tailors and carpenters are here regarded as "own account" workers, see Appendix V.

(14) Other "own account" workers include sawyers, leather workers, blacksmiths, goldsmiths, skilled building workers, local food preparers, etc.

(15) These totals include small numbers in occupations other than those in columns (1) to (14).

The following figures of numbers in certain occupations supplement Table 2:

MIGRANT POPULATIONS

Ethnic Group	Included in Column (7)	Included in Column (14)
1. "Akwapim"	"Fitters" 450, Electricians 350, "Longshoremen" 250	Building-workers 580, Sandal-makers 230, Blacksmiths 210
3. Ewe	"Fitters" 4,190, Sawyers 3,380 "Longshoremen" 1,380	Building-workers 8,180, Weavers 5,390, Blacksmiths 2,360, Goldsmiths 1,350
4. Krobo	Sawyers 830, "Longshoremen" 460, "Fitters" 310	Building-workers 510, Goldsmiths 260
5. Kwahu	"Longshoremen" 310, "Fitters" 300	Sandal-makers 320, Building-workers 250
7. Larteh		Building-workers 220
9. Atakpame		Building-workers 1,510
13. Dagarti	Loggers 300	
14. Fon		Building-workers 510
15. Frafra	Loggers 650	
16. Fulani	"Longshoremen" 360	
19. Hausa	"Longshoremen" 1,020, Fitters 220	Building-workers 290
20. Ibo	"Fitters" 300, Loggers 290	Building-workers 200
22. Kotokoli	"Longshoremen" 200	
23. Kru	"Longshoremen" 200	
27. Mossi	Loggers 1,820, Electricians 270, "Longshoremen" 210	
29. Songhai (Gao)	"Longshoremen" 630	
32. Yoruba	"Fitters" 550, "Longshoremen" 310	Building-workers 480, Goldsmiths 410, Carpenters 240
33. Zabrama	"Longshoremen" 770	

THE OCCUPATIONS OF MIGRANTS IN GHANA

TABL

OCCUPATIONS OF MALE

Ethnic Group	Food Farmers (1)	Cocoa Farmers (2)	Farm Labourers (3)
Southern Ghanaians			
1. "Akwapim"	12	39	5
2. Anum-Boso	11	42	4
3. Ewe	27	(15)	(5)
4. Krobo	42	27	3
5. Kwahu	5	45	3
6. Kyerepon	22	40	7
7. Larteh	13	39	4
8. Shai	16	47	7
Northern Ghanaians and Non-Ghanaians			
9. Atakpame	(..)	n.a.	34
10. Bawle	(..)	—	39
11. Builsa	74	—	6
12. Busanga	38	—	24
13. Dagarti	62	—	15
14. Fon	7	—	19
15. Frafra	57	—	12
16. Fulani	13	—	41*
17. Grusi, n.e.s.	14	—	38
18. Gurma, n.e.s.	8	—	70
19. Hausa	8	—	4
20. Ibo	3	—	3
21. Konkomba	95	—	3
22. Kotokoli	20	—	37
23. Kru	4	—	(..)
24. Kusasi	74	—	17
25. "Kyamba"	26	—	49
26. Lobi	78	—	18
27. Mossi	15	—	52
28. Pilapila	9	—	62
29. Songhai (Gao)	3	—	7
30. Wala	65	—	4
31. "Wangara"	12	—	37
32. Yoruba	5	n.a.	4
33. Zabrama	10	—	14
34. "Other Nigerians"	7	—	4

*Including herdsmen 21 percent.
See Notes on next page.

MIGRANT POPULATIONS

FTEEN YEARS AND OVER
(rcents)

Mine Labourers (4)	"Other Employees" (5)	Professional/ Clerical (6)	Traders (7)	Other "Own Account" (8)
—	8	15	3	14
—	7	10	3	18
—	11	7	2	20
—	7	5	2	9
—	6	11	9	15
—	6	8	2	12
—	5	12	4	20
—	8	5	(. .)	13
—	6	4	—	53
—	(. .)	(. .)	(. .)	20
(. .)	16	1	(. .)	1
2	28	—	2	4
4	13	1	—	2
—	22	(. .)	(. .)	39
3	21	1	2	2
1	22	2	7	9
2	34	1	2	3
2	14	—	1	3
2	25	4	21	26
8	45	6	19	13
—	1	...	—	—
1	19	1	10	10
4	69	(. .)	(. .)	4
—	6	—	—	1
—	12	1	3	6
—	(. .)	—	—	—
2	20	1	3	4
2	10	2	7	7
4	41	—	34	10
4	11	2	3	6
3	24	2	5	10
4	10	5	48	20
5	26	1	28	14
3	32	7	20	18

(continued on next page)

TABLE 3 (Footnotes continued)

Notes: — (. .) percentages omitted being based on figures under 100.

(i) See Notes on Table 2, the statistics being derived from the same source.

(ii) Columns (1) and (2) = Total in Farming. Columns (3) + (4) + (5) = Total in Employment (excluding Professional/Clerical). Columns (7) + (8) = Own Account Workers.

(iii) The percentages all add up to less than 100 owing to the omission of a few occupations such as fishermen, livestock and poultry keepers, palm wine tappers, etc., which did not fit conveniently into the classification.

Explanation of Column Headings

(2) See Appendix V. In the cases of all the Southern Ghanaian ethnic groups, all those shown under the census heading "farmers and farm managers (cocoa)" are here regarded as being cocoa farmers, as the proportion of *abusa* (labourers) is certainly very small—except possibly with the Ewe, which is why the percent is (in parentheses). With the Northern Ghanaian and Non-Ghanaian ethnic groups, all those "in cocoa" are here regarded as *abusa* (labourers) and are, accordingly, included in column (3), though it is realised that there were probably a few cocoa farmers among the Atakpame, Hausa and Yoruba populations. Unfortunately the total number of labourers employed primarily on cocoa farming cannot be estimated as the census classification "farm workers and agricultural labourers" must surely include non-*abusa* labourers on cocoa as well as food farms.

(3) All farm labourers, including *abusa* labourers. See, also, notes on column (2).

(4) "Diamond diggers," being regarded as "own account" workers are not included. (See Notes on Table 2.)

(5) See Notes on Table 2, column (7). It should be noted that general labourers (column [4] of Table 2) and "service" occupations (column [6] of Table 2) are included here.

(6) See Notes on Table 2, column (8).

(7) See Notes on Table 2, column (9).

(8) See Notes on Table 2, column (14) and also Appendix V. The percentages in this column are based on the figures in columns (10) to (14) inclusive of Table 2.

TABLE 4

MIGRANTS IN SIX NORTHERN GHANAIAN ETHNIC GROUPS
(Estimated Number of Occupied Males Fifteen and Over)

Occupations	Builsa		Busanga		Dagarti		Frafra		Kusasi		Wala	
	Mi-grants	Home-land	Mi-grants	Home-land	Mi-grants	Home-land	Mi-grants	Home-land	Mi-grants	Home-land	Mi-grants	Home-land
Abusa Cocoa labourers	150	—	1,280	—	1,430	—	570	—	1,850	—	170	—
Other farm labourers	800	(50)	3,140	—	5,900	160	3,960	100	3,900	(70)	320	(30)
Farm employment	950	(50)	4,420	—	7,330	160	4,530	100	5,750	(70)	490	(30)
General labourers	1,550	100	3,690	(50)	4,500	700	5,350	300	1,200	190	770	130
"Service"	850	—	1,070	(40)	730	200	1,800	120	260	160	160	(50)
Mining labourers	(90)	—	330	—	2,060	—	1,240	—	(50)	—	440	—
Other employment	160	—	310	—	400	(40)	710	(60)	140	(30)	160	(70)
Non-farm employment	2,650	100	5,400	(90)	7,690	940	9,100	480	1,650	380	1,530	250
Food farmers	—	13,020	—	6,910	—	31,680	660	22,000	—	25,600	200	7,560
Other	400	300	780	630	790	2,220	1,210	1,980	240	580	680	1,130
TOTAL	4,000	13,470	10,600	7,630	15,810	35,000	15,500	29,560	7,640	26,630	2,900	8,970

Note: — Figures under 100 are put in parentheses as a reminder of the sampling procedure.

(Notes continued on next page)

Notes on TABLE 4

The overall estimates in this table are reasonably reliable (assuming a sufficient reliability of the published census statistics) especially in those cases where the ethnic group in question makes up a substantial proportion of the total population of the homeland as defined below. The numbers of migrants were estimated by deducting the number of males in the local authority areas within which the homeland lay from the total numbers for the ethnic group—the former statistics being extracted from Table 7 of Census Report, Volume IV. The margin of error in the small figures is, of course, extremely high (see footnote 4). For occupational definitions see notes on Tables 2 and 3 and Appendix V. See also Part II.

Builsa

The Builsa homeland lies within the Builsa, Kassena-Nankani and S. Mamprusi local authority areas, but as over 90 percent of the Builsa in the North live in the Builsa local authority area, the proportionate occupational pattern in the homeland was based on that area. The assumption that all Builsa food-farmers are in the homeland appears very reasonable, given the total number of food-farmers in the Builsa local authority area.

Busanga

The Busanga homeland in Ghana lies within the Kusasi and S. Mamprusi local authority areas; mainly the former. Busanga people comprise about 16 percent of the total population of Kusasi: applying this percentage to the total of 39,052 food-farmers in Kusasi, there would be about 6,300 Busanga food-farmers there, so that it seems reasonable to assume that all Busanga food-farmers are in the homeland. As a high proportion of Busanga migrants originated outside Ghana, the above-defined homeland applies to a proportion, only, of the migrants working farther south.

Dagarti

The Dagarti homeland is in the Wala, Lawra and Tumu local authority areas. No outstandingly "heroic" assumptions lie behind these estimates.

Frafra

The Frafra homeland is in the Frafra, S. Mamprusi and Kusasi local authority areas. The number of food-farmers in the homeland was estimated as x percent of the total number of food-farmers in the Frafra local authority area (x being the percent of the total population of that area which is Frafra) plus 12 percent to allow for the fact that that proportion of Frafra was enumerated elsewhere in the North.

Kusasi

The Kusasi homeland is in the Kusasi and S. Mamprusi local authority areas, mainly the former. Kusasi people accounted for 58 percent of the total population of the Kusasi local authority area and the occupational pattern is based on that area. It seems reasonable to assume that all Kusasi food-farmers are in the homeland.

(continued on next page)

(TABLE 4 Notes continued)

Wala

The Wala homeland is in the Wala, Lawra and Gonja local authority areas; mainly the former. As Wala people make up only about a quarter of the total population of the Wala local council area, some of these estimates are less reliable than most of those for other ethnic groups. This should not, however, appreciably affect the totals of migrants and non-migrants.

SECTION 3

THE GEOGRAPHICAL DISTRIBUTION OF THE MIGRANT POPULATION

Twenty-nine of the thirty-four ethnic groups are here divided into five classes based on the geographical distribution of the migrant population, each of the remaining five ethnic groups having unclassifiable special characteristics. The classification is based on Table S1 in *Tribes in Ghana*—"Population by Local Authority of Enumeration and Tribe." The "three cities" are Accra, Kumasi and Sekondi-Takoradi.

(a) Migrant population mainly concentrated in rural areas most accessible to the homeland.

Krobo	(4)
Kwahu	(5)
Bawle	(10)
Konkomba	(21)
Lobi	(26)

(b) Migrant population mainly concentrated in cocoa districts

Anum-Boso	(2)
Kyerepon	(6)
Larteh	(7)
Shai	(8)
Gurma	(18)
Kotokoli	(22)
Kusasi	(24)
"Kyamba"	(25)

(c) Migrant population mainly concentrated in cocoa districts, with more than 10 percent in the three cities

"Akwapim"	(1)
Pilapila	(28)
"Wangara"	(31)

(d) Migrant population very widely dispersed throughout Ghana with less than a quarter in the three cities

Ewe	(3)	Fulani	(16)
Atakpame	(9)	"Grusi"	(17)
Builsa*	(11)	Wala*	(30)
Dagarti*	(13)	Yoruba	(32)
Fon	(14)	Zabrama	(33)
Frafra*	(15)		

*Based on the estimates in Table 4.

(e) Migrant population very widely dispersed throughout Ghana with more than a quarter in the three cities

Builsa*	(11)
Busanga*	(12)
Hausa	(19)
Zabrama	(33)

*Based on the estimates in Table 4.

Other unclassifiable

Ibo (20) Over half of the total population is in the Western Region, and nearly a quarter in the Accra Capital District.

Kru (23) They are mainly seamen concentrated in Sekondi-Takoradi and Accra.

Mossi (27) About three-quarters of all Mossi are in Ashanti, the North and Brong-Ahafo, where they are extremely widely dispersed—the largest concentration being in Kusasi (over 10% of the total). But there are some Mossi "nearly everywhere" in Ghana.

Songhai (Gao) (29) The 29 percent of all Songhai who live in rural areas are mainly in West Akim Abuakwa and in rural Ashanti and Brong-Ahafo.

"Other Nigerians" (34) The distribution of "Other Nigerians" is very similar to that of the Ibo.

SECTION 4

URBANIZATION

There is very great variation as between ethnic groups in the extent to which migrants work in rural, as distinct from urban, areas. Many variables account for this, including deliberate preferences for farming (or other rural work), historical migratory patterns, costs of transport and the willingness of migrants to enter employment proper. Thus, some peoples, such as the Krobo (4), are reluctant to migrate except as farmers, despite the proximity of their homeland to Accra and other urban centres. Second, many migrants join their "brothers" or "countrymen," wherever they may happen to have established themselves in past decades. Third, some migrants, such as the farmers denoted as "seeping migrants" in Section 2, could not in any case afford to incur transport costs, so that they never travel far from their homeland. Fourth, members of some migrant groups are quite unprepared to work in employment (proper) in urban areas, for instance as general labourers, building and construction workers or as domestic servants. Naturally, as will be seen, there is a close association between the general occupational pattern, as classified in Section 2, and the degree of urbanization.

All localities with a population of 5,000 or more were regarded, for census purposes, as "urban" and were often referred to as "towns." Nearly a quarter (23%) of the total Ghanaian population was recorded as being urban, of whom nearly half were in the three cities - Accra, Kumasi and Sekondi-Takoradi.

Southern Ghanaians

Table 5 relates to the urbanization of the eight Southern Ghanaian "migratory ethnic groups." The relative degree of urbanization of migrants cannot be assessed from column (1); first because there is much variation in the extent of urbanization in the homeland (for instance nearly all Larteh people resident in the homeland are urbanized), and second because of variations in the proportions of migrants in the total population.

A convenient rough measure of "municipalization" (if not of urbanization) is provided by column (4) of Table 5 which shows the estimated percentages of migrants enumerated in the three cities (in fact mainly in Accra for these ethnic groups). Using this measure,

TABLE 5

DEGREE OF URBANIZATION: SOUTHERN GHANAIAN "MIGRATORY ETHNIC GROUPS"
(In Percents)

Ethnic Group	Percent of Total Population			Percent of Migrants
	In Urban Areas (1)	In the Three Cities (2)	Estimated as Resident in the "Homeland" (3)	Estimated as Resident in the three Cities (4)
Kwahu (5)	27	10	70	33
Ewe (3)	22	9	(65)	(26)
"Akwapim" (1)	25	11	25	15
Anum-Boso (2)	21	4	30	8
Krobo (4)	9	2	(73)	(7)
Larteh (7)	37	3	33	4
Shai (8)	6	3	30	4
Kyerepon (6)	7	1	43	2

Explanation of Column Headings

(1) Urban areas are localities with populations of 5,000 or more.
(2) The three cities are Accra, Kumasi and Sekondi-Takoradi.
(3) The "homelands" were defined as the following local authority areas: Kwahu (South and North Kwahu), Ewe (Volta Region), "Akwapim" (Akwapim and Nsawam), Anum-Boso (Anum-Boso/Akwamu), Krobo (Manya-Yilo-Osodoku), Larteh (Akwapim), Shai (Ga-Dangbe-Shai), Kyerepon (Akwapim).
(4) Estimated from columns (2) and (3).

The percentages in parentheses are very rough.

the Kwahu and the Ewe are the most urbanized followed by the "Akwapim." Migrants belonging to the other four ethnic groups are little urbanized.

Northern Ghanaians and Non-Ghanaians

The most urbanized of the Non-Ghanaian ethnic groups are the Kru, the two Songhai-speaking groups and the four Nigerian groups: as Table 6A shows, this is true in terms of the proportions in both urban areas and the three cities. High proportions of all these peoples were born outside Ghana and migrants (however defined) are clearly highly urbanized. All these ethnic groups, save the Yoruba and the Zabrama, are concentrated rather in cities than in other urban areas.

TABLE 6A

DEGREE OF URBANIZATION: NORTHERN AND NON-GHANAIAN "MIGRATORY ETHNIC GROUPS"
(In Percents)

Ethnic Group	Percent of Total Population			Percent Males Born Outside Ghana (4)
	In Urban Areas (1)	In Three Cities (2)	In Urban Areas Excluding Three Cities (3)	
Kru (23)	73	64 (Sek)	9	80
Songhai (Gao) (29)	71	54 (Ksi)	17	94
Ibo (70)	63	51 (Sek, Acc)	12	80
Hausa (19)	61	35 (Acc, Ksi)	26	56
"Other Nigerians" (34)	53	36 (Acc)	17	71
Yoruba (32)	49	21 (Ksi, Acc)	28	62
Zabrama (33)	46	29 (Acc)	17	87
"Wangara" (31)	35	15 (Acc, Ksi)	20	50
Fon (14)	33	17 (Acc, Ksi)	16	81
"Grusi," n.e.s. (17)	32	19 (Ksi, Acc)	13	23
Fulani (16)	31	19 (Acc, Ksi)	12	61
Kotokoli (22)	25	10 (Acc)	15	47
Mossi (27)	21	10 (Ksi, Acc)	11	72
Pilapila (28)	20	18 (Sek, Acc)	2	46
Bawle (10)	(19)	Neg.	(19)	61
Gurma (18)	17	9 (Acc, Ksi)	8	42
"Kyamba" (25)	16	10 (Acc)	6	36
Atakpame (9)	11	3 (Ksi)	8	77
Lobi (26)	2	Neg.	Neg.	45
Konkomba (21)	1	Neg.	Neg.	5

Note: — "Neg." = negligibly small.

See notes on Table 5.

Column (2) The main city (or cities) is shown in brackets: Acc is Accra, Ksi is Kumasi and Sek is Sekondi/Takoradi.

See, also, Table 6B.

About a third of all "Wangara," Fon, Grusi and Fulani are urbanized: the proportion in the three cities is lower, in each case, than with the seven most urbanized groups.

The least urbanized ethnic groups are the Lobi and Konkomba, the percentages of urbanization being two and one respectively.

Urbanization percentages for the six Northern Ghanaian ethnic groups that were treated separately in Table 4, are here shown in

TABLE 6B

DEGREE OF URBANIZATION:
SIX NORTHERN GHANAIAN ETHNIC GROUPS
(In Percents)

	Percent of Total Population in Urban Areas (1)	Percent of Total Population in Three Cities (2)	Crude Relative Index of Propensity of Migrants to Work in Cities (Busanga = 100) (3)
Busanga (12)	25	19	100
Builsa (11)	9	6	94
Frafra (15)	14	6	53
Wala (30)	27	3	56
Dagarti (13)	6	2	30
Kusasi (24)	4	1	22

See notes on Table 5.

Column (3) This index is based on the ratio of the total population (male and female) in the three cities to the estimated total number of occupied migrant males. The numbers of migrant females cannot be estimated.

Table 6B. As the estimated proportions of migrants in the total populations are so variable, the percentages in Column (1) of this table do not indicate the relative propensity of migrants to congregate in urban areas. Also, not all those resident in towns are migrants, Wa in the Wala homeland being a town. The crude index shown in column (3) refers to the relative propensity of migrants to work in cities: Busanga and Builsa migrants are clearly more apt to work in cities than migrants belonging to the other four ethnic groups.

SECTION 5

SUMMARY OF PRECEDING STATISTICS

The main conclusions of Sections 2, 3 and 4 are summarized in Table 7, which speaks for itself.

TABLE 7

SUMMARY TABLE: OCCUPATIONS AND
GEOGRAPHICAL DISTRIBUTION OF MIGRANTS

Occupational Classification of Migrants (Section 2) (1)	Urbanization Percentages (2)	Geographical distribution of migrant population (3)
(i) The migrant food-farmers		
Krobo (4)	Very low	Mainly concentrated in rural areas near homeland
Konkomba (21)	Very low	Mainly concentrated in rural areas near homeland
Lobi (26)	Very low	Mainly concentrated in rural areas near homeland
(ii) The migrant cocoa-farmers		
"Akwapim" (1)	Average	Mainly in cocoa areas, more than 10% in 3 cities
Anum-Boso (2)	Average	Mainly in cocoa areas
Kyerepon (6)	Very low	Mainly in cocoa areas
Larteh (7)	Very low for migrants	Mainly in cocoa areas
Shai (8)	Very low	Mainly in cocoa areas
(iii) The migrant farm-labourers		
Gurma (18)	Rather low	Mainly in cocoa areas
Kusasi (24)	Very low for migrants	Mainly in cocoa areas
"Kyamba" (25)	Rather low	Mainly in cocoa areas
Mossi (27)	Average	Very widely dispersed
Pilapila (28)	Average	Mainly in cocoa areas, more than 10% in 3 cities
(iv) The general urban and rural proletariat (excluding miners)		
Builsa (11)	Average for migrants	Very widely dispersed more than 25% in 3 cities
Busanga (12)	Rather high for migrants	Very widely dispersed more than 25% in 3 cities

TABLE 7 (continued)

Occupational Classification of Migrants (Section 2) (1)	Urbanization Percentages (2)	Geographical distribution of migrant population (3)
Fulani (16)	Rather high	Very widely dispersed, less than 25% in 3 cities
Grusi (17)	Rather high	Very widely dispersed, less than 25% in 3 cities
Kotokoli (22)	Average	Mainly in cocoa areas
"Wangara" (31)	Rather high	Mainly in cocoa areas, more than 10% in 3 cities
(v) As (iv) including miners		
Dagarti (13)	Rather low for migrants	Very widely dispersed, less than 25% in 3 cities
Frafra (15)	Not clear	Very widely dispersed, less than 25% in 3 cities
Wala (30)	Not clear	Very widely dispersed, less than 25% in 3 cities
(vi) Traders and "own account"		
Yoruba (32)	Very high	Extremely widely dispersed, less than 25% in 3 cities
(vii) Non-farming employment		
Ibo (20)	Extremely high	Mainly in Western Region of Accra
(viii) Traders, "own account" and non-farming employment		
Hausa (19)	Extremely high	Very widely dispersed, more than 25% in 3 cities
Songhai (Gao) (29)	Extremely high	About half in 3 cities
"Other Nigerians" (34)	Very high	Mainly in Western Region and Accra

TABLE 7 (continued)

Occupational Classification of Migrants (Section 2) (1)	Urbanization Percentages (2)	Geographical distribution of migrant population (3)
(ix) Occupational specialists		
Atakpame (9)	Very low	Very widely dispersed, less than 25% in 3 cities
Fon (14)	Rather high	Very widely dispersed, less than 25% in 3 cities
Kru (23)	Extremely high	Mainly in Sekondi/Takoradi and Accra
(x) Miscellaneous		
Ewe (3)	Average	Very widely dispersed, less than 25% in 3 cities
Kwahu (5)	Average	Mainly concentrated in rural areas near homeland
Bawle (10)	Not clear	Mainly concentrated in rural areas near homeland

Explanation of Column Headings
(1) Ethnic groups are classified according to Section 2 above.
(2) The degree of urbanization is that of the total population unless there are explicit references to migrants. Urbanization percentages significantly above or below 23 percent (the average for the total Ghana population) are regarded as high or low (see Section III).
(3) These estimates relate to the distribution of the migrant population resident outside the homeland, as defined in Part II.

SECTION 6

THE SEX RATIO OF THE MIGRANT POPULATIONS

Although as discussed in *Tribes in Ghana,* there are many unexplained anomalies affecting census sex ratios, the relative propensity of certain northern Ghanaian wives to migrate to urban areas with their husbands is roughly indicated by the sex ratio statistics in Table 8—the Wala have been omitted since Wa town is itself large enough to count as "urban."

The following points may be noted concerning sex ratios for the non-Ghanaian ethnic groups. See Table 9:

TABLE 8
NORTHERN GHANAIAN ETHNIC GROUPS

Ethnic Group	Number of Males Per 100 Females		
	Urban	Rural	Total
Builsa (11)	179	96	101
Konkomba (21)	130	101	102
Dagarti (13)	178	101	104
Frafra (15)	166	100	106
Kusasi (24)	141	107	108
Busanga (12)	147	126	130

TABLE 9
NON-GHANAIAN ETHNIC GROUPS

Ethnic Group	Number of Males Per 100 Females		
	Urban	Rural	Total
Kotokoli (22)	93	99	97
"Kyamba" (25)	97	103	102
Pilapila (28)	99	107	105
"Other Nigerians" (34)	107	112	110
Lobi (26)	187	111	112
Yoruba (32)	114	117	116
Atakpame (9)	124	124	125
"Wangara" (31)	140	124	129
Busanga (12)	147	126	130
Ibo (20)	149	183	161
Hausa (19)	146	197	163
Grusi (17)	155	168	164
Kru (23)	159	198	169
Bawle (10)	...	...	171
Fon (14)	...	...	179
Fulani (16)	257	183	202
Mossi (27)	213	309	284
Gurma (18)	296	311	308
Zabrama (33)	441	573	506
Songhai (Gao) (29)	1,404	381	827

(*a*) The very high proportion of females in the Kotokoli, "Kyamba" and Pilapila populations whose homeland in each case is northern Togo or Dahomey.

(*b*) The high proportion of females in the "Other Nigerian" and Yoruba populations, despite the length of the journey to

Ghana; this is, no doubt, associated with the high proportions of women belonging to these ethnic groups who are occupied in Ghana, see Section 7.

(c) The proportion of females in the Hausa population is much lower than that in the Yoruba population despite the many points of comparison between these two migratory groups and the fact that the Hausa have been migrating to Ghana on a considerable scale for many decades.

(d) The low proportion of females in the Fulani, Mossi and Gurma populations: in the case of the Gurma this is certainly associated with a preference for short-term spells of rural employment, not exceeding a year.

(e) The very low proportion of females in the Zabrama and Songhai (Gao) populations—these people are the seasonal, or short-term, migrants par excellence.

(f) The high ratio for the Grusi is of doubtful reliability considering that only 23 percent of all Grusi males were recorded as born abroad.

SECTION 7

THE OCCUPATIONS OF MIGRANT WOMEN

As the statistics do not enable the occupations of women resident in the Ghanaian homeland to be distinguished from those of women residents elsewhere, this Section relates to the 19 Non-Ghanaian ethnic groups only.

As Table 10 shows, there is very great variation between ethnic groups in the extent to which women are recorded as occupied. Nearly three-quarters of all Yoruba women are so recorded—a much higher proportion than for any other ethnic group. High proportions are also recorded for the "Other Nigerians," the Pilapila and the Hausa.

Little significance attaches to the low percentages: as is pointed out in *Tribes in Ghana* (p. lxxii) the instruction to take account of whether a woman worked as a farmer in the farming season (the census was held on 20th March in the dry season) was clearly widely ignored by enumerators in the North.

In any case, much the most important occupation of migrant women is trading, as Table 10 shows. For eleven ethnic groups more than half of all occupied women were recorded as being traders. As for the Yoruba, 91 percent of all occupied women were recorded as being traders, very high percentages also being recorded for the Hausa (86%), Ibo (81%) and Zabrama (78%).

There are few other occupations in which more than 10 percent of occupied women are engaged; however 23 percent of "Other Nigerian" occupied women are in service occupations and 23 percent of Pilapila occupied women are cocoa-labourers, presumably often working alongside their husbands.

TABLE 10

FEMALE OCCUPATIONS

Ethnic Group	Percent Of All Females (15 and Over) Recorded As Occupied	Percent Of All Occupied Females	
		Traders	Any Other Occupation Comprising Ten Percent or More
Yoruba (32)	70	91	—
"Other Nigerians" (34)	51	51	"Service" 23
Pilapila (28)	47	51	Cocoa-labourers 23
Hausa (19)	42	86	—
Atakpame (9)	41	41	—
"Kyamba" (25)	38	41	Food-farmers 23 "Cocoa" † 14
Kotokoli (22)	38	64	Food-farmers 11
"Wangara" (31)	35	55	Cocoa-labourers 13
Songhai, including Zabrama (29 & 33)	31	78*	—
Ibo (20)	31	81	—
Fulani (16)	23	60	—
Mossi (27)	22	44	Food-farmers 20
Grusi (17)	21	53	—
Gurma (18)	15	(48)	...
Lobi (26)	13	6	Food-farmers 61 Food-labourers 10
Kru (23)	Neg.	(35)	...
Bawle (10)	Neg.	(33)	...
Fon (14)	Neg.	(64)	...

*Zabrama women only—the number of Songhai (Gao) occupied women being negligible.
†Some cocoa-farmers may be included.

II

NOTES ON THE THIRTY-FOUR "MIGRATORY ETHNIC GROUPS"

IN the following reference notes on the 34 "migratory ethnic groups," the 8 southern Ghanaian groups are listed first, followed by the 26 Northern Ghanaian and non-Ghanaian groups.

The notes on each ethnic group are arranged in three paragraphs:

Paragraph *(a)* is mainly concerned with briefly interpreting the definition of "tribe" adopted in the census, with special reference to the "homeland." The principal authority is Westermann *et al.* (1952) the most useful source, although the authors were involved in a linguistic classification. A very practical approach has been adopted. The census figures on "tribe" exist: these notes are merely brief aids to their interpretation.

Paragraph *(b)* mainly relates to the occupational pattern of males and should be read in conjunction with Tables 2 and 3 where much more detail is provided. It should be noted that all *percentages* (and other proportions) in this section necessarily relate to the total population of occupied males aged 15 and over and not to migrants only; wherever possible, broad estimates of the *numbers* of *migrant* males in different occupations are made.

Paragraph *(c)* deals, very briefly, with the geographical distribution of each ethnic group within Ghana. Again it should be remembered that these percentages necessarily relate to the *total* (male and female) population in Ghana, not to migrants only.

As will be apparent to readers, somewhat more detail is provided for certain of the ethnic groups on which the author has special knowledge than in the general run of cases.

See also the list of References and Appendix I.

SOUTHERN GHANAIAN ETHNIC GROUPS

1. "Akwapim" (Akuapem)

a) Denoted as Akwapim in the census (and here denoted as "Akwapim"), this curious "tribe" consists neither of the inhabitants of the whole state of Akwapim (for the Kyerepon and the Larteh are classified separately), nor solely of *Akan* Akwapim (as is explicitly stated) for the inhabitants of Mampong and Mamfe, for instance, who are included are not of Akan origin, though they now speak Twi. However, for practical purposes, "Akwapim, other than Larteh and Kyerepon" is a geographically distinct group, though heterogeneous ethnically (see Hill, 1963). The "Akwapim" statistics were probably inflated by the inclusion of some Larteh and Kyerepon respondents who denoted themselves "Akwapim" without qualification. It may here be noted that many other "tribes" are "curious" in a manner similar to the Akwapim—there having always been mobility and migration—but that in many instances the knowledge enabling us to make detailed comments of this type is lacking.

b) For over 70 years the inhabitants of the Akwapim state have been migrating as cocoa-farmers, mainly to Akim Abuakwa, but also to many other districts (see Hill, 1963). Two-fifths (39%) of all males were recorded as being cocoa-farmers; all of them migrants in the sense that they probably spend much of their time away from Akwapim, where nowadays there are few cocoa-farmers. The "Akwapim" have a higher percentage of males in the "professional/clerical" group (15%) than any other "migratory ethnic group." The Ga (who are not considered "migratory") are the only other ethnic group in Ghana with a higher percentage (21%), but if only professional and administrative occupations are included (clerks being omitted) the "Akwapim" easily head the Ghanaian list. More than four-fifths of those in this "professional etc." work are migrants outside Akwapim. The other main male occupations are "self-employed" 14 percent (of whom 5% are drivers) and food-farmers 12 percent (nearly all in Akwapim).

c) Only about a quarter of the total "Akwapim" population lives in the homeland; the remainder live, dispersedly, throughout Ghana (except in the North), about 8 percent of the total being in Accra.

2. Anum-Boso

a) The Anum-Boso (who are matrilineal Guan people) now inhabit two towns (populations 4,301 and 2,588) in southern Ghana near the Volta lake.

b) The history of the Anum-Boso as migrant cocoa-farmers is

"MIGRATORY ETHNIC GROUPS" 37

dealt with in Hill, 1963. Their occupational pattern is very similar to that of the Larteh. (See also, "Akwapim.") About a third of the population lives in the homeland: nearly all those who stated they were food-farmers probably reside there. Over two-fifths of adult males (42%) were recorded as being cocoa-farmers.

c) As migrant cocoa-farmers the Anum-Boso are more widely dispersed than the Larteh, but less than the "Akwapim": there is a high concentration of them in Asamankese (see Hill, 1963) where there was a "mass migration" to a former "homeland" some fifty years ago.

3. Ewe

a) The Ewe homeland extends from southern Dahomey, through Togo, to southeastern Ghana. It was perhaps unavoidable that the very heterogeneous group comprising the "tribe" of Ewe speakers ("Ewe" is merely a language group) should have been treated as a whole for census purposes (only the Fon being distinguished separately). This means, however, that the very different patterns of migration of different branches of the group stand unrevealed by the statistics. The total population of 872,860 Ewe comprises the second largest "tribe" in Ghana, being exceeded only by the Ashanti (895,360).

b) The Ewe propensity to migrate is much greater than is superficially indicated by the high proportion (two-thirds) of the population which is resident in the "homeland", for this homeland has necessarily to be defined as the Volta Region, within which there is much migration and into which there is immigration from Togo. (See, in this connection, the note on Table 1.) The main difficulty in handling the figures is that some branches of the Ewe group are very much more mobile than others and have special manners of migration—for instance as sea, or river fishermen. The failure to distinguish cocoa-farmers and *abusa* labourers is here very serious. With most ethnic groups one would not go far wrong in assuming that all those recorded as connected with cocoa-farming are either farmers or *abusa*, but with the Ewe this is not so and it is impossible to indicate, even roughly, the proportion of the 28,180 men "in cocoa" which is likely to be cocoa-farmers.

Although the Ewe are unique in the extreme diversity of the capacities in which they migrate (this being reflected, in their widespread dispersion throughout Ghana, see [*c*] below), this is of little significance given the "ethnic heterogenity" of this linguistic group. Certain Ewe are apt to migrate as food-farmers to southern Ghana, renting land temporarily and always being liable to move away—some 8,000 of the 51,400 Ewe food-farmers might be farming outside the

Volta Region. One-fifth (20%) of all occupied men are "self-employed": principally carpenters, building workers, weavers and tailors. Nearly a third of all those in Ghana who designated themselves as carpenters were Ewe and perhaps about a half of the Ewe carpenters were migrant. The Ewe migrant is found in most types of employment, even including mining (400 cases recorded). Seven per cent of all occupied males are fishermen.

c) The Ewe are urbanized to an average degree, 22 percent. They are found in every city, comprising 15 percent and 5 percent of the populations of Accra and Kumasi. There are some Ewe living in every one of the 69 local authority areas; outside the North there were only 5 (out of 55) such areas with fewer than 1,000 Ewe.

4. Krobo

a) The original Krobo homeland (proper) lies in the plains west of the Volta River, north of Akwapim, but for a century or more Krobo farmers have been migrating northwards into the hills, companies of men purchasing the land outright and jurisdiction over the uplands ultimately passing to the two Krobo states (see Hill, 1963). The propensity of these people to migrate is not, therefore, correctly indicated by the proportion (73%) of Krobo who are resident in the "Homeland" (which is necessarily defined as the whole of the Manya-Yilo-Osudoku council area) for only about 15 percent of all Krobo live in the five main towns on the plains. The original Krobo system of migration, which involved the meticulous division of the purchased land into strips, was possibly unique in Africa.

b) Although cocoa was at one time planted on many of the strip-farms in Upper Krobo, it has nearly all died (not necessarily of swollen shoot) and the land is again mainly devoted to food-farming and the oil palm, this being reflected in the very high percentage of men (42%) who were recorded as being food-farmers. The proportion of men (27%) who stated they were cocoa-farmers (including *abusa*) must surely be an over-estimate, there being little cocoa in the homeland where (see above) 73 percent of the total population was enumerated. The Krobo participated in the westward migration into Akim country (Hill, 1963), where most of their cocoa-farms are situated. Many of the Krobo "own account" workers were recorded as being carpenters and building workers, probably mainly working in the homeland. Nearly a quarter of those in "other employment" are sawyers.

c) Krobo migrants are much less widely dispersed than the "Akwapim." Few Krobo migrate except in the capacity of farmers (or *abusa*) and most of those who are farming outside Krobo country are in Akim. The Krobo are little urbanized.

5. Kwahu (Kwawu)

a) The Kwahu are an Akan people whose homeland lies northeast of Akim, bordering Ashanti. Their propensity to migrate is higher than the proportion of 70 percent resident in the homeland would suggest, there being much migration, especially of cocoa-farmers, within the Kwahu homeland.

b) Although some of the 45 percent of all males who were occupied in cocoa-farming were probably *abusa* men (Hill, 1956), it is still worth noting that the percentage of cocoa-farmers and *abusa* is higher than for any other southeastern ethnic group except the Shai. Most of these cocoa-farmers (and *abusa*) farm in Kwahu country, including a few on the remote Afram plains. The low proportion recorded as being food-farmers is partly explained by the fact that most food-farming in this, as in most other Akan societies, is done by women, but also, presumably, reflects the farmers' preference to denote themselves as cocoa-farmers if they produce any cocoa at all. The Kwahu have for long had a high propensity to migrate in non-farming occupations, mainly as traders and craftsmen (tailors and sandal-makers)—see Garlick (1967). The early establishment of mission schools in the uplands of Kwahu is reflected in the high proportion (9%) in "professional/clerical" jobs.

c) The Kwahu are nearly as widely dispersed as the "Akwapim," except that there are relatively fewer of them in the Western Region. As with the "Akwapim," 8 percent of them reside in Accra. There are very few Kwahu in the North.

6. Kyerepon

a) The Kyerepon, who are patrilineal Guan people with a distinct language, mainly inhabit a number of towns in northeastern Akwapim, including Adukrom, which is here, rather arbitrarily, regarded as their "homeland." It is probable, see "Akwapim" above, that some Kyerepon are included under the "Akwapim" heading in the census.

b) The occupational pattern for men is similar to that of the "Akwapim," though food-farmers account for as many as 22 percent of occupied males (mostly in the homeland) and fewer men are "professional/clerical."

c) More Kyerepon than "Akwapim" reside in the homeland (43 percent against 25 percent). As migrant cocoa-farmers they are much less widely dispersed than the "Akwapim," most of their cocoa-farms being in Akim country. They are also much less urbanized, notably few of them living in Accra.

7. Larteh

a) The Larteh, who are patrilineal Guan people with a distinct language, are the inhabitants of a town of that name on the Akwapim ridge (population 6,381). See "Akwapim" and Hill, 1963. Some Larteh people are probably included under the "Akwapim" heading.

b) The occupations of the Larteh people are similar to those of the "Akwapim," though the proportion of "professional/clerical" is lower; of "own account" workers higher.

c) Like the Kyerepon, the Larteh, as migrant cocoa-farmers, are much less widely dispersed than the "Akwapim." There are very few of them in Accra.

8. Shai

a) The Shai homeland is in the Accra plains south of the Akwapim ridge, Dodowa being the main town (Hill, 1963). Like their neighbours the Krobo, the Shai are patrilineal Adangme people.

b) The Shai are outstanding migrant cocoa-farmers. No cocoa grows in the homeland and nearly all the 47 percent of all men who were recorded as cocoa-farmers (only a few are likely to have been *abusa*) were probably migrants. Most of those who were recorded as being food-farmers were presumably at home: indeed few Shai migrate except in connection with cocoa. (Only about 590 Shai were enumerated in nearby Accra.)

c) As migrant cocoa-farmers the Shai are not nearly as widely dispersed as the "Akwapim," nearly all of them being in southern Akim country.

NORTHERN AND NON-GHANAIAN ETHNIC GROUPS

9. Atakpame

a) Given their failure to break down certain huge "ethnic groups," such as the Ewe, it is curious that the census authorities should have regarded the people of the town of Atakpame in Togo, who are said to be predominantly Yoruba-speaking, as a "distinct tribe," for there are many other larger groups better qualified for such special treatment.

b) However, the statistics are interesting in revealing that the Atakpame are occupationally more specialized than any other group listed here, over half of all the occupied men in Ghana being "building workers," presumably mainly rural house-builders. It is impossible to judge whether most of the 20 percent of all occupied men who were recorded as having a connection with cocoa-farming are *abusa*: perhaps they are, as the only other occupation of any importance is farm labouring (13%)—presumably mainly in cocoa.

c) As building workers and cocoa-farm labourers the Atakpame are very widely dispersed throughout the country, except in the North.

10. Bawle (Baule)

a) Immigrants from the Ivory Coast, the Bawle are an Akan people.

b) The statistics are unclear and the sample is small, but it is probable that the Bawle mainly immigrate as cocoa-farmers and cocoa-labourers, this being their pattern of migration in the Ivory Coast (see Dupire, 1960).

c) Nearly all the Bawle in Ghana are in western cocoa-farming districts, near the Ivory Coast.

11. Builsa

a) The Builsa (also known as Kanjaga, a town-name) are classified in the census as Mole-Dagbane people, though Westermann (1952) regards them as Grusi, and Fortes (1945) states that their language is unintelligible to Mole or Dagbane speakers. Rattray (1932: 398) is right in referring to them as a "hotch-potch people created by local migrations and counter-migrations and intermarriage of clans belonging to both the Moshi [Mossi]-speaking group and to the Kasen-Isal-speaking group." The various towns had little in common until they were administratively grouped by the British. The Builsa homeland is near the northern frontier of Ghana, south of Navrongo, where about 85 percent of them reside, including virtually all those enumerated as food-farmers.

(*b*) It is estimated in Table 4 that about a fifth of all occupied males work outside the homeland. Of these about 40 percent work as general-labourers, 25 percent as farm-labourers and 22 percent are in the service industries, more than half of them as policemen. Few Builsa are in mining.

c) As general and agricultural labourers and as policemen, Builsa migrants are widely distributed throughout Ghana, perhaps about a quarter of them being in Kumasi and about a tenth in Accra.

12. Busanga

a) The Busanga should be regarded as partly immigrant and partly indigenous, 28 percent of those enumerated in Ghana having been born abroad, mainly in Upper Volta, which country according to

Manoukian (1951), who quotes unpublished information received from D. Tait, is their "principal" homeland. Of the total of Busanga males who were born abroad, 29 percent were enumerated in the North, 28 percent in Ashanti and 16 percent in Accra. Over 90 percent of all the Busanga in the North are in Kusasi in the extreme northeast, most of the remainder being in south Mamprusi. The Busanga comprise only about 16 percent of the total Kusasi population.

b) It is estimated in this paper that about 58 percent of all occupied males are migrants, in the arbitrary sense that they are at work in districts outside northern Ghana, so that those who have migrated from Upper Volta to Kusasi are not regarded as migrants. About 42 percent of these migrants are farm-labourers (of whom about 12 percent are *abusa*) and about 35 percent are general-labourers. About 10 percent are in "service" occupations. Only 3 percent are mining labourers and 2 percent sales workers.

c) As general and agricultural labourers the Busanga mainly work in Ashanti, Brong-Ahafo and Accra, though there are some in the cocoa districts of the Eastern region. Otherwise they are heavily concentrated in Kumasi and Accra, where 17 percent of all the Busanga in Ghana were enumerated.

13. Dagarti (Dagarte or Dagaba)

a) The Dagarti, who are Mole-Dagbani people, are mainly Ghanaian indigenes, but some 6 percent of them were recorded as being immigrants into Ghana, mainly, so far as the record goes, from Upper Volta and the Ivory Coast. The probability is, however, that most of those recorded as originating in the Ivory Coast were in fact Lobi, in which case their actual country of origin is likely to have been Upper Volta (see Lobi). Rattray (1932: 404) regarded the Dagarti (who ought to be called the Dagoba) as of "very mixed stock, comprising under this name elements which were formerly Isala, Lobi, Wala and possibly others." While it may be generally stated that the Dagarti homeland lies in northwest Ghana, north of that of the Wala, many Dagarti live in the Wala local authority area (as defined in 1960), the boundary of which was drawn to include the southern part of the Dagarti homeland. The Dagarti comprise 81 percent of the population of the Lawra council area further north.(See also, Wala).

b) It is estimated (Table 4) that about a third (31%) of all Dagarti occupied males are migrants in the sense that they work in districts outside the Wala, Lawra and Tumu local council areas. Nearly one-half (46%) of these migrants are estimated to be farm-labourers of whom 9 percent are *abusa*, 28 percent of them are general-labourers and 13 percent are mining-labourers—as much as 14 percent of the total Ghanaian employment in mines. Therefore nearly 9 out of 10 of all migrant males are in these three types of labouring employment.

c) As farm, general and mining labourers the Dagarti are widely dispersed throughout Ghana, though there are relatively few in the Eastern and Volta regions.

14. Fon

a) The Fon, whose homeland is in southern Dahomey, speak an Ewe dialect. Four-fifths of them (81%) were recorded as born outside Ghana.

b) Fon men (like the Atakpame, though not to the same degree) are specialist rural house-builders when in Ghana, about a third of them being so engaged. Their other main occupations are farm labouring (19%) and general labouring (11%).

c) As building-workers, farm-labourers and general labourers, the Fon are remarkably widely dispersed, considering their small numbers, except in northern and eastern Ghana.

15. Frafra

a) As ethnographers tend to identify the Kankansi (or Gurense) with the Frafra (see Fortes, 1945, and Westermann, 1952, though the latter states that the Kusasi are also known as Frafra), and as the Frafra are not mentioned at all in the "ethnological synopsis" in *Tribes in Ghana*, it is necessary, for present purposes, to define the Frafra as the main inhabitants of the Frafra local authority area which is in the extreme northeast of Ghana, west of the district inhabited by the Tallensi, the Nankansi (or Gurense) then being the main inhabitants (other than the Kasena) of the Kassena-Nankani local authority area further west. Whether this "geographical distinction corresponds to a real ethnic distinction must remain a matter of doubt. It appears certain that some migrant Tallensi must have designated themselves as Frafra, for the recorded proportion of Tallensi migrants appears far too low.

b) It is estimated in this paper that about two-fifths (39%) of Frafra occupied males are migrants who work outside the homeland. About one-third of these migrants (34%) are general-labourers; of the remainder, farm-labourers account for 29 percent (of which about an eighth are *abusa* men), mining labourers account for about 8 percent and the "service" occupations for about 12 percent (of whom about half are in domestic service). Frafra migrants have a number of other miscellaneous occupations, including logging, and are far from being specialists.

c) Mainly in their capacities as general, farm and mining labourers, the Frafra are widely dispersed throughout Ghana, except in the Volta and Eastern regions; about half of them are in Ashanti and Brong-Ahafo.

16. Fulani

a) The Fulani, who speak a great variety of different dialects, are scattered over a vast area of West Africa from Senegal to Mauretania (in the west) to Cameroon (in the east). As is confirmed by the low ratio of females in the Fulani population, in most parts of Ghana the Fulani should be regarded as immigrants, 61 percent of males having been born abroad, the principal countries of origin being Upper Volta, Mali and Niger. But only 31 percent of the male Fulani enumerated in Northern Ghana were born abroad, many Fulani having been settled there for generations, especially in Kusasi in the extreme northeast.

b) Far from being mainly pastoralists (as popular belief so often supposes) the Fulani in Ghana pursue a multitude of different occupations and are highly urbanized. (This diversity of occupation partly reflects the great "ethnic diversity" of those Fulani who seek work in Ghana.) About one-fifth (21%) of all occupied males are concerned with cattle; most of them presumably in charge of herds mainly owned by others, though in the Kusasi-Mamprusi area there may be more herd owners. One-fifth (20%) are farm-labourers, nearly a fifth of them *abusa*. Food-farmers, most of them presumably in northern Ghana, account for 13 percent of all occupied males. Other occupations are general-labourers 10 percent, sales workers 7 percent and "service" 7 percent.

c) Apart from the concentration of Fulani in the extreme north (Kusasi, Mamprusi and Lawra districts), the notable fact about the geographical distribution of the Fulani is that they are found nearly everywhere, seldom in concentrations of any size. See Rouch, 1956.

17. "Grusi", n.e.s.

a) This ragbag "ethnic group" is said (*Tribes in Ghana*) to comprise "Grusi people" other than the Mo, the Vagala, the Sisala and the Kasena and it is certainly to be distinguished from all of them (except the Mo) in the low proportion (only a quarter) enumerated in the north. According to *Tribes in Ghana* the Lela, the Nunuma and the Tampolensi are included, together with other unspecified Grusi. The "Grusi" (as thus defined) are partly immigrant into Ghana (23 percent of males were recorded as born abroad) and are largely migrant from northern Ghana southwards: only 19 percent of all "Grusi" males

"MIGRATORY ETHNIC GROUPS" 45

were enumerated in the north, compared with 57 percent who claimed to have been born there. Although for the purposes of this monograph the "Grusi" have been tentatively classified as "non-Northern-Ghanaian," a distinction ought to be drawn between the Tampolensi, who have been in Ghana since time immemorial, and the much more numerous Awuna Grushi whose homeland straddles the northern frontier and who are the main migrants to the south. (In fact, the term "Grusi" makes sense only as an "objective classifier" for a certain family of languages.)

b) The proportion of migrant "Grusi" cannot be estimated, but presumably the 14 percent of occupied males who said they were food-farmers were all, or mostly, farming in their "homeland." Farm-labourers account for about 43 percent of the total of all occupied males (exclusive of food-farmers), the corresponding proportion for general-labourers being 25 percent, for all other types of "employment" 17 percent.

c) The "Grusi" are found everywhere in Ghana, except in the southern Volta Region, there being no large conglomerations except in Kumasi and Accra.

18. Gurma, n.e.s.

a) In *Tribes in Ghana* it is stated that this ragbag conglomeration consists first of the Barba (Bariba) and the Kambera and second of all other Gurma who are not Pilapila, Kyamba, Konkomba or Bimoba. There must be something wrong about the inclusion of the Barba because these peoples are to be identified with the Pilapila (See Pilapila below) and because virtually none of those classified under this heading are recorded as originating in Dahomey, the home of the Barba. Rouch (1956) states that the Gurma of Ghana have two homelands and should be regarded as separate groups: these are the districts of Fada n'Gourma (Upper Volta) and Dapango (Northern Togo). In Froelich *et al.* (1963) it is noted that there are Gurma in the extreme north of Togo. The census statistics showing country of origin include the Bimoba with the Gurma: but they do show that Togo must be the principal country of origin of the Gurma, followed by Upper Volta.

b) Ragbag ethnic grouping though this appears to be, the classifiction "Gurma" is yet highly significant occupationally. Ghanaian cocoa-farmers are apt to regard Gurma labourers as the specialist annual labourers par excellence, a fact which corresponds first with the relatively low percentage of all Gurma farm-labourers who are classified as *abusa* (31% compared with 51% for Pilapila), and second with the very high sex ratio of the Gurma (308) compared with the

Pilapila (105), the point being that annual labourers (unlike *abusa*) are not accompanied by their wives. As many as 70 percent of all occupied male Gurma are farm-labourers, the remainder including: general-labourers 8 percent, "service" 4 percent, mining labourers 2 percent.

c) Over a half of all the Gurma are in Ashanti and Brong-Ahafo, mostly in the cocoa districts, and nearly a fifth are in the cocoa districts of the Eastern region. Some Gurma are found in nearly every local authority area, except in the south of the Volta region.

19. Hausa

a) Any Hausa-speaking person of northern Nigerian origin, irrespective of whether he happens to be of Fulani descent (though pastoral Fulani are an exception), is likely to denote himself "Hausa," as are Hausa-speakers from Niger (see, also, Zabrama). A small proportion of Hausa stated that they had been born in other countries (in particular Upper Volta) from where, presumably, they had earlier migrated. Although as many as 56 percent of all male Hausa stated they they had been born abroad, there are many Hausa whose fathers or grandfathers were the original settlers in Ghana. There are also many, though the census can tell us nothing of this, who have been settled so long in Northern Ghana as to denote themselves "Dagomba," "Wala," etc. (See Appendix III).

b) The Hausa in Ghana are in many different types of occupation. If butchers and meat sellers (10% of all occupied males) be regarded as "sales" workers, then this latter category accounts altogether for nearly one-third (31%) of all occupied males; about 11 percent are farm-labourers (most of them in cocoa) and about 10 percent general-labourers; food-farming accounts for as much as 11 percent and "service" occupations for 7 percent.

c) The Hausa are very highly urbanized, nearly a third of the total living in Kumasi or Accra. But those who do not live in the big cities are greatly dispersed (mainly in small towns) and there are only three local authority areas in Ghana, where, as estimated in the census report, there are fewer than 100 Hausa.

20. Ibo (Igbo)

a) Ibo-speaking peoples of Eastern Nigeria. Four-fifths (80%) of the males, that is, nearly all the adults, were recorded as having been born abroad.

b) About a half (52%) of all Ibo occupied men are in a variety of types of non-farming employment, in "service" industries (mainly domestic service), as general or mining labourers, as loggers, etc. About a fifth (19%) of all Ibo men are traders. Only three percent of all Ibo men are farm-workers. As many as 6 percent are in "professional/clerical" jobs.

c) The Ibo are very highly urbanized (63%). Some special factor (such as that formerly their long journey was always made by sea to Takoradi) must partly explain their high concentration in the Western region, where over 50 percent of them were enumerated. There are very few Ibo in the Volta, Brong-Ahafo and Northern regions.

21. Konkomba

a) The Konkomba of Ghana (these Gurma people are also found in Togo) live in the northeastern part of the country, principally in Eastern Dagomba, Nanumba, Eastern Gonja and Buem-Krakye. They are included in this list of migratory peoples, not because the census statistics track their mobility, but because they are known from other evidence, notably Tait (1961), to be "highly mobile on the ground." They are pressing fast westward out of the Oti plain, an area of severe soil exhaustion, "into a great triangle of formerly unoccupied territory between Salaga, Bimbila and Krakye." They are "seeping migrants."

b) The Konkomba migrate as farmers, some of them growing yams and other foodstuffs for commercial sale. As many as 95 percent of adult males were recorded as being food-farmers; a much higher proportion than for any other of the 34 ethnic groups.

c) Only 1 percent of all Konkomba are "urbanized." The only district outside the expanding area of their "homeland" where there is any significant concentration of Konkomba, is Sekyere, where they may be either cocoa or food-labourers rather than farmers.

22. Kotokoli (Tem)

a) Although the name Kotokoli is repugnant to social anthropologists both because of its imprecision and because, according to Froelich *et al.* (1963), its etymology is obscure (these authorities would presumably not regard it as a name "given" by Hausa, as does Westermann), it is yet a term which, like Frafra, cannot be dispensed with. It would appear that all Tem speakers from the *cercle* of Sokode in northern Togo are classified as Kotokoli in the census, and certainly the principal country of origin is Togo. Although nearly a half (47%) of all the male Kotokoli in Ghana were born abroad, yet as many as 17 percent of the male population were recorded as being "Ghanaian" (see Appendix III), most of them probably having been enumerated in the Volta, Eastern and Ashanti Regions.

b) Nearly two-fifths (37%) of Kotokoli men work as farm-labourers, probably mainly in cocoa—there may be a few cocoa-farmers among them. A fifth of Kotokoli men (20%) are otherwise employed, mainly as general-labourers and longshoremen—Kotokoli do not work in the mines. One-tenth (10%) of Kotokoli are traders, in particular, kola-traders. Whether the Kotokoli migrate in the first instance as food-farmers, in which occupation 20 percent are engaged, is not known. The 10 percent of Kotokoli recorded as working on their own account are mainly drivers, diamond-diggers and tailors. The recorded percentage of "unemployment" among Kotokoli men (10%) was higher than for any other ethnic group—whether an appreciable proportion was genuinely without (though seeking) work, and if so why this should be, are matters on which there is no information.

c) Nearly a third of all the Kotokoli enumerated in Ghana are in Buem-Krakye (in the Volta Region), whence they migrate from their nearby homeland, the men presumably mainly working in cocoa, though some must be in food-farming. Other rural concentrations are Kumasi (north and west) and West Akim Abuakwa - these people tend to coagulate rurally. Nearly a tenth of all Kotokoli live in Accra and Kumasi, mainly the former, where they presumably mostly work as labourers and traders.

23. Kru

a) The name Kru was originally employed by Europeans to denote a number of coastal peoples, mainly Liberians, who speak related dialects.

b) The fact that the Kru are famed as seamen does not emerge from the census occupational statistics, most of those who work at the ports, or in ships, being classified as "general labourers"; this heading, together with longshoremen, account, however, for only 52 percent of all occupied males. Other main occupations are "service" 14 percent, farm-labourers 5 percent, food-farmers 4 percent.

c) The Kru are heavily concentrated in Sekondi-Takoradi (the nearest port to their homeland) where 36 percent were enumerated; at the time of the census, when the surf-boats were still operating at Accra, 27 percent of the Kru population was at that port. About nine-tenths of all Kru were enumerated in either the Western region or the Accra Capital District.

24. Kusasi

a) The Kusasi are Mole-Dagbani peoples whose homeland is in the extreme north-east of Ghana as well as in adjoining districts of

Upper Volta, though only 1 percent of all Kusasi males in Ghana had been born abroad. These people comprise 58 percent of the total population of the Kusasi local authority area.

b) It is estimated (Table 4) that about one-fifth (22%) of all Kusasi men are migrants in the sense that they are working elsewhere than in the Kusasi or Mamprusi local council areas. About three-quarters (75%) of all Kusasi migrant males are farm-labourers, most of them probably in cocoa. The only other occupation of importance is "general labour," which accounts for about 16 percent.

c) Kusasi migrants are mainly concentrated in the cocoa areas of Ashanti and Brong-Ahafo.

25. "Kyamba"

a) The "Kyamba" group of Gurma-speaking peoples would have been better denoted here as the "Bassare." The group as defined in the census includes the Bassare, who as migrants are certainly far more numerous than the Kyamba proper—from whom they are quite distinct, though both groups originate in northern Togo. (According to Froelich *et al.* [1963], about a quarter of all the Bassare of Togo are apt to be in Ghana at any time, many of them making long stays there, and this proportion may even be an under-estimate.) Although the "Kyamba" are here classified as a basically immigrant people (36% of the males were recorded as born abroad), yet as many as 33 percent of the males were recorded as being "Ghanaians" (see Appendix III).

b) About half (49%) of all adult males are farm-labourers, probably mainly in cocoa; about a quarter (26%) were recorded as being food-farmers, which probably means that migrant "Kyamba" are often farmers. The other principal occupation is general labouring (8%).

c) Rurally-enumerated "Kyamba" are concentrated principally in the north, in Buem-Krakye, where they percolate relatively easily from their Togo homeland, probably as farmers as well as cocoa-labourers, and in the cocoa-growing districts of Ashanti and Brong-Ahafo, as well as in certain parts of the Eastern Region. About 8 percent of the total population is in Accra.

26. Lobi

a) The census is erroneous in recording the principal country of origin of the Lobi in northwest Ghana as the present Ivory Coast - in actuality it is mainly Upper Volta (which was part of the Ivory Coast when many of the immigrants were born.) The Birifor were included with the Lobi, though the census-takers later regretted this.

Although the omnibus term "Lobi" embarrasses most anthropologists, see Goody (1956), it need not embarrass us here. The Lobi are the principal immigrant peoples of northwest Ghana, the migration being currently in full flood. If, as is possible, many of these immigrants pass themselves off as Dagarti, especially in some localities, the statistics relating to their occupational and geographical distribution will be somewhat misleading. The seeping eastward migration of the Lobi over the Black Volta is a migration of farming "families". Superficially, at any rate, it resembles that of the Konkomba on the other side of Ghana, though it has got up momentum more recently, mainly since 1948. Immigrant Lobi remain permanently in Ghana, where their general migratory movement continues, whole compounds removing, or sections hiving off. Even if their migration from Upper Volta was mainly caused by increased pressure on the land, this is not necessarily the main cause of their continuing migration within northern Ghana.

b) Although in his new Ghanaian homeland the Lobi man has few occupations other than food-farming (supplemented by cattle-raising), he is much more inclined to migrate onward as a farm-labourer than is his eastern "counterpart" the Konkomba — 18 percent of all adult males being employed as farm-labourers, most of them probably in cocoa. The Lobi are employed only to a trivial extent as general-labourers or in any other non-agricultural occupation, unless (see above) they then denote themselves Dagarti. As many as 78 percent are occupied as farmers, a proportion which in this list is exceeding only by the Konkomba.

c) The Lobi, who are in process of seeping in from Upper Volta as farmers, were mainly enumerated in the Wala, Western Gonja and Lawra local authority areas. Those who work as cocoa-labourers are nearly all in Brong-Ahafo, the cocoa district nearest their homeland. Their urbanization percentage is extremely low.

27. Mossi

a) The Mossi being the largest mainly immigrant group in Ghana, with a total population of 106,140, one would wish to know whether, in practice, the census-takers had much difficulty in identifying the numerous separate branches of this ethnic cluster. There is also the question of the extent to which those individual Mossi who have been long-settled in Ghana prefer to denote themselves members of a Ghanaian-based ethnic group. Nearly three-quarters (72%) of the male Mossi enumerated in Ghana were recorded as born abroad. There is probably a substantial population of settled Mossi in Northern Ghana, but unfortunately the particular census statistics relevant to this question do not distinguish the Mossi separately. Skinner (1960) notes that many Mossi fled to Ghana from Upper Volta to avoid forced labour.

"MIGRATORY ETHNIC GROUPS" 51

b) Dupire (1960) has designated the Mossi in cocoa-farming districts in southeastern Ivory Coast as representing a "rural proletariat." In Ghana over half (52%) of Mossi occupied males are farm-labourers, about a quarter of whom are *abusa*, some of the remainder perhaps being labourers in food-farming; about 15 percent are food-farmers, who are presumably the principal representatives of the settled Mossi population. One-fifth (21%) of all Mossi are in non-farming types of employment, more than half of whom are general-labourers.

c) Nearly a quarter of all Mossi were enumerated in the Northern region, of whom nearly a half were in Kusasi. About a half of all Mossi are in Ashanti and Brong-Ahafo, mostly in rural districts. There are not many Mossi in the southern cocoa districts, except in Kwahu and there are very few in the Volta region. Mossi are well represented in the western region.

28. Pilapila

a) According to Westermann (1952) the Pilapila are Gurma people from northwestern Dahomey, especially from the Djougou district in which case they may be known as Zugu. According, however, to an unpublished paper by Lombard (1961), the Zugu (who are the original inhabitants of Djougou) are to be distinguished from the Bariba or Pilapila. This is most confusing as the "Barba" of the census are presumably to be identified with the Bariba and are classified under Gurma n.e.s. (see above). A further difficulty is that less than half of all the male Pilapila enumerated in Ghana who had been born abroad, gave their birthplace as Dahomey, nearly a third having been recorded as born in Togo and nearly a fifth in Upper Volta. Lombard notes that the Zugu were early migrants to the Gold Coast, where they became well assimilated thanks to their old contacts with the Hausa, and a remarkably high percentage of "Pilapila" were recorded as of "Ghanaian origin" (see Appendix III). It may be that most Pilapila are Zugu; certainly Lombard regards most northern Dahomean migrants as such.

b) Whoever the Pilapila may be, their high degree of occupational specialization is certainly noteworthy, nearly two-thirds (62%) of occupied males are farm-labourers; half of them *abusa*, and most of the remainder probably are ococa-labourers; about a tenth (9%) of them are food-farmers, which suggests that some Pilapila migrate as farmers. As many as 7 percent are traders, this high percentage distinguishing them from other Gurma peoples.

c) As cocoa-labourers the Pilapila are mainly concentrated in Ashanti, Brong-Ahafo and Buem-Krakye, with a sprinkling in Kwahu and Akim Abuakwa. It would seem that as traders they are mainly in Accra. Few Pilapila are resident in Kumasi, and there are scarcely any Pilapila in the Northern Region.

29. Songhai (Gao)

a) Songhai-speaking people inhabit the region of the upper Niger bend from Djenne in the west to the borders of Nigeria in the east. This group, which is defined in the census as consisting of all Songhai who are not Zabrama (see Zabrama), is probably mainly composed of those who count themselves "Gao." This does not, however, mean that their homeland is near the town of that name since Rouch (1956) defines the "Gao" as including Songhai-speakers from circles and sub-divisions Issaber, Goundam, Timbuctoo, Gourma-Rharous, Bourem, Gao, Ansongo, as well as Bella, Moors and Touaregs! He notes that the migration of two groups of Songhai-speaking people into Ghana (the Zabrama and the Gao) reflects "the great schism of their history," the descendants of the Songhai conquered by the Moroccans in the sixteenth and seventeenth centuries being denoted as Gao. The Gao (as this group will now be denoted) are perhaps the most transient of all immigrants into Ghana: 94 percent of all males were born abroad; 62 percent of them in Mali, 18 percent in Niger and 16 percent in Upper Volta.

b) A third (34%) of all occupied male Gao are traders, a higher percentage than for any other ethnic group except the Yoruba. Their other principal occupations are longshoremen 17 percent, "services" 12 percent, general-labourers 11 percent, farm labourers 7 percent.

c) Two-fifths of all the Gao in Ghana live in Kumasi and about 10 percent in Accra, the Gao being more urbanized (71%) than any other immigrant group except the Kru. Such Gao as live in rural areas are mostly in Ashanti, Brong-Ahafo and Akim. There are no Gao in the Volta or Northern regions.

30. Wala

a) The Wala are a heterogeneous group of Mole-Dagbani people of northwest Ghana, whose name is derived from the town Wa. They are scarcely an ethnic group (see Rattray, 1932, and also, Dagarti above). Over three-quarters (77%) of Wala were enumerated in the homeland; most of them were in the Wa local council area, with a few in the Lawra and Western Gonja areas. Some Dagarti aspire to denote themselves as Wala, or were denoted as such by the enumerators when they were landowners in Wa.

b) It is estimated in this paper that about a quarter (24%) of all adult males are migrants working outside the homeland, this on the assumption that all those Wala who gave their occupation as "food-farmer" were in northern Ghana and a few of them elsewhere than in the homeland. The principal occupations are general-labourers (accounting for about a quarter [27%] of all migrants), farm-labourers (17%, probably mainly cocoa) and mining labourers (15%).

c) As cocoa, mining, and general labourers, the Wala migrants are fairly evenly distributed throughout the country, except in the Volta region. About 10 percent of all the Wala enumerated outside the homeland were in Kumasi, about 4 percent in Accra.

31. "Wangara"

a) The census tribe Wangara is here denoted as "Wangara" to convey that the usage of this portmanteau name is full of pitfalls (see, in this connection, Wilks, 1961: 162-63, and Goody, 1964). In the census Wangara is defined as consisting of three groups of Mande-speaking people, the Bambara, the Dyula and the Mandingo: this definition presumably derives from Westermann (1952: 33) who notes that this tripartite "dialect cluster" must, linguistically, be considered such, in spite of the vast areas over which the languages are spoken and the variety of "dialectal subdivisions." According to Paques (1954), the chief country to which the Bambara of the French Sudan migrated was the Gold Coast. Over half (57%) of all the "Wangara" enumerated in Ghana who were born abroad, were recorded as originating in Upper Volta (many, presumably, from Bobo-Dioulasso), the other principal countries of origin were the Ivory Coast (18%) and Mali (14%). There are settled communities of "Wangara" in some parts of Ghana, for example Cape Coast. The uncertainties affecting the name Wangara, which is sometimes identified with Dyula (Dioula), are not peculiar to Ghana: even anthropologists in the southern Ivory Coast are apt to denote any northern Muslim trader, at times any northern Muslim, as Dyula (Dioula). Many settled Wangara in places such as Wa or Bole presumably conceal their origin for census purposes, describing themselves as Wala or Gonja.

b) Most "Wangara" occupied males are recorded as being in employment as farm-labourers (38%—certainly mainly cocoa), general-labourers (13%), and in other occupations (14%). As only 5 percent of "Wangara" denoted themselves as "traders" there must have been massive concealment of trading interests on the part of those immigrants who do not count themselves Bambara, few of whom would be prepared to work as labourers.

c) Over a half (59%) of all "Wangara" in Ghana were enumerated in Ashanti or Brong-Ahafo, most of them in the cocoa districts;

few of them (only 6% of the total) in Kumasi. A fifth of all "Wangara" are in the Western Region, where they are widely distributed.

32. Yoruba

a) Quite unsuitably, the Yoruba are grouped with the Ibo in certain less detailed tables in *Tribes in Ghana* and the proportion of Yoruba originating in Nigeria (presumably almost entirely in Western Nigeria) has to be estimated—it is about 89 percent, Togo and Dahomey being the other main countries of origin. In Ghana the Yoruba people are often denoted as "Lagosians" and, wishing to fall in with local usage, even those immigrants whose homeland is far from Lagos may refer to themselves as such. Presumably all "Lagosians" were classified as "Yoruba" in the census (according to the census lists "Lagos" is one of 16 separate branches of Yoruba), but whether some who hail from "Lagos" and who call themselves Lagosians are in fact Hausa, or other non-Yoruba, is not known. Nearly two-thirds (62%) of all Yoruba males enumerated in Ghana were born abroad, this precentage varying little between regions.

b) Nearly a half (48%) of all Yoruba adult males designated themselves as engaged in selling or trading, a far higher proportion than for any other ethnic group. A high, though unknown, proportion of these "traders" was presumably in cocoa-buying, though after 1960 the cocoa-buying authorities sought, perhaps somewhat unsuccessfully, to eliminate the Nigerian middleman's traditional role of buying directly from cocoa-farmers on their farms. A considerable proportion of Yoruba traders may have been concerned with "collecting" other produce, such as maize, or *gari*, directly from farmers. As a general rule the Yoruba man in Ghana eschews wage *employment* though 4.5 percent of occupied men are engaged as mine labourers, 3.5 percent as farm labourers, 3 percent as general labourers. One-fifth (20%) are engaged in work on their own account (other than trading), of which tailoring and diamond-digging account for more than half.

c) The geographical distribution of the total Yoruba population in Ghana more closely resembles that of the total Ghanaian population than does that of any other single ethnic group, though there are proportionately more Yoruba in the Eastern region and fewer in the Volta and Northern regions. Nearly 10 percent of all the Yoruba enumerated in Ghana were in Kumasi and about 8 percent were in Accra; but as so many Yoruba traders work in rural areas the degree of urbanization (49%) is lower than for some Nigerian peoples such as the Ibo.

33. Zabrama

a) The Zabrama (or Zarma), see Westermann (1952), consist of many branches of Songhai-speaking peoples whose home is in the Niger Republic along the stretch of the Niger River extending from the neighbourhood of Niamey to the Nigerian frontier: Rouch (1956) lists (i) the "pure" Songhai of Tillabery-Niamey, (ii) Zerma of Tillabery-Niamey-Dosso, (iii) Kurtey of Tillabery, (iv) Woggo of Tillabery, (v) Dendi of the circle of Dosso, (vi) Bella of Tillabery (see also Songhai above). However, according to the census, only about half (49%) of the male Zabrama enumerated in Ghana were born in Niger, 28 percent having been born in Upper Volta and 11 percent in Mali. Owing to the difficulty in ascertaining a Zabrama man's country (as distinct from town) of origin, these figures may understate the percentage born in Niger. Alternative hypotheses are that some Zabrama migrated to Ghana by way of Upper Volta and other countries, which seems, however, unlikely to have occurred on any scale, as these people's migratory system usually involves short term oscillations between their homeland and their place of work, or that many Songhai peoples who are not true Zabrama prefer to denote themselves as such, or were so denoted by baffled enumerators. The Zabrama population in Ghana is very large in relation to that in the homeland; but as it is known to be transient, it is reasonable that 87 percent of males should have been recorded as having been born outside Ghana, compared with 94 percent of the other (far less numerous) group of Songhai-speaking peoples (see [*c*] below). For reasons of internal politics in Ghana, many Zabrama probably denoted themselves "Hausa."

b) As many as 28 percent of occupied male Zabrama (compared with 34 percent of other Songhai) were classified as traders. Their other principal occupations are general-labourers and farm-labourers (each 15%), and diamond-diggers and food farmers (each 10%). As long-distance migrants the Zabrama are unusual in working in food-farming, as both labourers and farmers.

c) The geographical distribution of the Zabrama population in Ghana was so unlike that of other Songhai, that it seems that either there was some "real ethnic distinction" between the two groups (might the Zabrama have been all Songhai-speakers who did not denote themselves Gao?) or that the nomenclature varies as between regions. Therefore, only 6 percent of all Zabrama were enumerated in Kumasi compared with 40 percent of all other Songhai, the corresponding percentages for Accra being 22 percent and 10 percent. The geographical distribution of the Zabrama is extraordinarily widespread, with some of them in every local authority area except for a few in the North. Their urbanization percentage (45%) is lower than that of the other Songhai (71%).

34. "Other Nigerians"

a) Many minor ethnic groups are necessarily included within this residual category, so that it is a pity that no indication is given of the relative importance of some of the larger groups, notably the Ijaw.

b) The "Other Nigerians" pursue many different occupations, but they are not interested in farming. Traders account for 20 percent of the total of occupied males, "service" (of which about three-quarters are in domestic service) for 18 percent, diamond-diggers for 10 percent, general-labourers for 9 percent and "professional/clerical" for 7 percent, a higher percentage than for any other non-Ghanaian ethnic group, though little higher than for the Ibo.

c) Like the Ibo, the "Other Nigerians" are heavily concentrated in the Western region, 53 percent of the total population of each of these groups having been enumerated there. In each case, also, about a quarter of the population was enumerated in Accra. The only other major concentrations of these peoples are in the diamond-digging districts of Western Akim Abuakwa and in Kumasi. There are very few local authority areas, outside the North, without a sprinkling of "Other Nigerians."

APPENDIX I

NOTES ON THE CENSUS CONCEPT OF "TRIBE"

The general system of "tribal classification" adopted in the census is described in the introduction to *Special Report "E": Tribes in Ghana* as being "multipurpose." "Taking advantage of the available information and certain selected purposes of analysis, a classification under three criteria was adopted: these were language, traditional or historical classification and geographic affinity or origin" (p. xi). The whole classified list of tribes comprised 18 "first level" language groups (Akan, Ewe, Guan, etc.) one of which was "miscellaneous" or "other." Two of these major groups and the miscellaneous group were further subdivided into sub-groups, thus the Akan sub-groups were Nzema, Anyi-Bawle, Twi-Fante (Fante), Twi-Fante (Twi) and Akan n.e.s. (not elsewhere specified). At both these levels of classification "language" is said to have been the criterion, the only exception being the Twi-Fante. The third level of classification of the 92 "tribes" was partly in terms of language, but also in terms of the other two criteria; this still left some of the 18 "first level" groups undivided, for example the Hausa, the Fulani, the Ibo, while others, such as the Central Togo tribes, were divided into many groups.

Although *Tribes in Ghana* has an introduction of 110 pages, this includes no discussion of the practical difficulties encountered by enumerators in deciding on a person's tribe. According to the official Enumerator's Manual, enumerators were merely instructed to obtain from all African informants "what their tribe is and write it down in the space provided." It was added that "to assist you in writing down the correct spelling of the respondent's tribe, a list of tribes is given"—it was in an Appendix to the Manual.

This list of tribes which, it will be noted, existed merely to assit the enumerator's spelling, consisted of 142 names. While it formed the basis of the final published list of 92 tribes, there are a few names in the shorter list which are not in the longer one, understandably, as enumerators were not instructed to conform to the longer list in writing down "what informants said their tribe was."

Although *Tribes in Ghana* contains no mention of the kinds of difficulties encountered by informants in interpreting their instruction to write down the tribe to which the respondent said he belonged, another census volume, *General Report*, Vol. V, by B. Gil and K.T. de Graft-Johnson (which was published later than *Tribes in Ghana* added this (p. 115): "There is . . . . . the problem of classifying the children of Ga fathers and Akan mothers. It was decided by the Census Office that . . . . . the acceptance of the answer of the respondent himself could be taken as a simple approximation of tribal affiliation." It also confirmed that, though provided with a list of tribes, enumerators were "as a general rule . . . . instructed to write down in detail all the information given."

In *General Report* (Vol. V) it is explained that the "multi-criteria classification" referred to above, was adopted by the Census Office on its own responsibility, an attempt to work out an agreed classified list in conjunction with "interested lecturers of the University College of Ghana, as well as scholars in government departments" having earlier failed. ("The two meetings arranged for finding an acceptable basis for classification ended without results because the meetings got bogged down with questions of definition."[1]) However, during the processing stage of the census data in 1962 the code list was reexamined by a special committee, which included three linguists and one geographer from the University of Ghana, and one judges that, even at that late stage, it proved possible to amend the classification slightly. In Appendix A of *Tribes in Ghana* there is a long table entitled "Statistical and Language Classification compared" which resulted from the work of this special committee; it includes a few critical comments which should be useful to future census-takers.

After spending much time analysing the statistics relating to the occupational and geographical distribution of the 34 "migratory ethnic groups" to which this paper relates, I have concluded that the census-taker's practical approach towards "tribal classification" (an approach which leant so heavily on the commonsense of the enumerator) generally yielded much better results, so far as the present very limited purpose is concerned, than I had feared. By this I mean that the statistics showed much more internal consistency than I had expected and were generally in accord with the knowledge I had picked up during years of field work among both rural and urban migrants. However, the list of 34 ethnic groups did include a few, such as the "Pilapila" and the "Kyamba," which I found definitionally wholly baffling for reasons given under the appropriate headings in Part II which should be read in conjunction with this Appendix.

There were many matters, not all of them detailed, about which I felt critical, or where I felt doubt. Songhai-speaking peoples, for in-

---

[1] It is difficult to imagine what else they could have got bogged down with! As members of the staff of the University of Ghana are here explicitly criticized by Dr. Gil and his colleagues in the Census Office, the present writer wishes to record that although she was nominally a member of a Census Advisory Committee, of which the committee that got "bogged down" was an off-shoot, important constructive suggestions regarding classificatory questions which she made by letter on two occasions were totally ignored.

APPENDIX I

stance, were classified as Zabrama and "other": did the "other" group in fact largely consist of those normally denoted as "Gao" and who are the Gao? As a research worker I feel most grateful to the census authorities for publishing *Tribes in Ghana*, the "primary purpose" of which is stated to be that of giving "the research worker in the social sciences (especially the sociologist) a few basic data on population groups which are distinguished by certain characteristics and are generally referred to as tribes or tribal groupings." But the research value of the splendid material offered would have been much enhanced had the authorities provided some really practical information on the difficulties encountered at all stages. Admittedly, they are more forthcoming than most of those who prepare official national income estimates—estimates which are apt to be revised retrospectively in manners wholly unrevealed. Admittedly, too, the introduction to *Tribes in Ghana* includes some discussion, most of it mathematical, of the limitations of the data. What is missing, and what would have helped to allay or resolve numerous doubts and criticisms, is a discussion of the practical difficulties encountered by enumerators at the grass roots level. This would have been far more useful than the long "Ethnological Synopsis of the Major Tribes in Ghana," which is too generalized to be useful to research workers, and which fails to recognize the limitations of the anthropological material relating to many ethnic groups. Thus, to take an instance, little is known about that section of the "Lobi" who live in Ghana. It would have been most useful if there had been some discussion on the matter of how enumerators decided whether to classify a respondent as "Lobi": but a statement, in the ethnological synopsis, that there are "three recognized means of contracting a marriage among the Lobi" is useful to no one and unlikely to be reliable.

A practical difficulty which required discussion is one mentioned by Dr. Jean Rouch (1956) in his *Migration au Ghana*.

All the emigrants are known in the Gold Coast by traditional names having little connection with the real name of their ethnic group. But these names have passed so fully into usage that the emigrants themselves endorse these pseudo-nationalities: "Amadou Wangara," "Ali Gao," "Moukaila Zabrama." This is not a renunciation, even temporarily, of their true nationality. A "Zabrama" has not forgotten his ethnic group nor his village, but this is a matter for themselves, and for the strangers of the Gold Coast it suffices that they are "Zabrama" . . . . This taste for anonymity is one of the aspects of the behaviour of the emigrants to the Gold Coast, who, even when one knows them well, refuse to reveal their real name. Most of the travel documents that I have consulted give names such as "Japan," "Twopense" [*sic*] . . . or better still adopt as a family name the choicest insults of their language *(injures de leur langue)* [my translation].

This is a general obstacle to good census-taking of the highest importance and affects migrant northern Ghanaians as well as non-Ghanaians.

Another major difficulty is that respondents might happen to classify themselves in a general way rather than to particularize as expected by the census-takers. Thus some Larteh respondents might have referred to themselves as Akwapim, Larteh town being in that state; they would then be classified as Akwapim not as Larteh. This could have been corrected at the coding stage in respect to those resident in the homeland but not in respect to migrants: hence the propensity of the Larteh to migrate would tend to be underestimated in the census, while that of the Akwapim would be overestimated.

Of course any ethnic classification necessarily slurs over the matter of ethnic heterogeneity within groups, which is apt to be an especially serious problem with very large immigrant groups, such as the Mossi. The classification adopted by the census being multi-purpose, rather than solely linguistic, it is a pity no attempt was made to sub-divide a few of the larger groups, which are especially "heterogenous," on some kind of "political" or geographical basis. In his notes on the chief immigrant groups Rouch (1956) notes, for instance, that certain Fulani "stay separate" from others, that French Grusi are divided into three groups and have separate chiefs and that the Gurma of Fada n'Gourma (Upper Volta) and of Dapango (Togo) have "a tendency to separateness in the Gold Coast and to have distinct chiefs."

One possible reason for the "heterogeneity" of immigrant ethnic groups is that long-term and short-term migrants may be wholly indistinguishable statistically. Thus a Hausa butcher born in Ghana, whose grandfather had been "the first to migrate," would for most purposes be "added in with" a recently arrived Hausa trader who happened to have no intention of remaining away from home for long. In accordance with the census definition of "foreign origin" (see Appendix III) this grandson of the original immigrant as well as the newcomer would be classified as "foreign,"—that is, non-Ghanaian.

APPENDIX II

DEMOGRAPHIC ANTHROPOLOGY: MIGRATION ON MARRIAGE

The census statistics relating to the proportions of the population born in the locality in which they were enumerated are generally of little value, partly owing to the difficulty encountered by enumerators in handling the concept of locality (see Appendix IV). But as these difficulties presumably affected the enumeration of males and females alike, they would not seem to invalidate comparisons between the sexes. In fact, such comparisons do seem to indicate that among many Northern Ghanaian peoples a high proportion of women move to their husband's birthplace (which is different from their own) on marriage. In accordance with the findings of anthropologists, they also suggest that only in matrilineal (Akan) societies are husbands at all apt to move to their wife's birthplace on marriage.

The following statistics were drawn from Summary Table 3 of Volume II of the Report on the 1960 Ghana census. In order that they should relate as far as possible to the sedentary population (thus eliminating the complication that males have a higher propensity than females to migrate long distances), the statistics refer to local authority areas not to ethnic groups: for the same reason, the 40 local authority areas where more than 15 percent of the total population was born outside the region are omitted, so that the following figures refer only to 29 out of the total of 69 local authority areas.

There were altogether seven local authority areas, all in Northern Ghana, where a very much greater proportion of males than of females had been born in the locality where they were enumerated, these being:

PERCENTAGE BORN IN LOCALITY
WHERE ENUMERATED

Local Authority Area	Males	Females
Tumu	85	42
Kassena-Nankani	92	50
Frafra	92	57
Builsa	95	68
Lawra	80	56
Wala	75	51
Western Dagomba	71	54

There were only four local authorities, all Akan, where an appreciably greater proportion of females than of males had been born in the locality where they were enumerated, these being:

PERCENTAGE BORN IN LOCALITY
WHERE ENUMERATED

Local Authority Area	Males	Females
Brong-Ahafo North	72	78
Kumasi South	74	80
Amansie	61	65
Asin	58	64

For seven of the remaining eighteen local authority areas, the corresponding male ratio was appreciably higher than the female ratio: all these areas were either in Northern Ghana or on the coastal fringe, where the population is basically patrilineal. Of the remaining eleven areas, where the ratios were approximately equal, six were areas mainly inhabited by matrilineal Akan.

(See Oppong [1967] for an analysis, based on the 1960 census, of intra-regional mobility by ethnic group, with reference to indigenous economic and political systems, modes of reckoning descent and marriage and socialization practices.)

APPENDIX III

THE "FOREIGN ORIGIN" POPULATION

"Country of origin" was defined in the census as follows:

> The country of birth of father/mother and of grandfather/grandmother of respondent depending on whether one or both parents were born in Ghana and on whether a matrilineal or patrilineal approach is adopted in determining tribal allegiance (Tribes in Ghana, p. xxv).

As most of the 34 "migratory ethnic groups" are "patrilineal" this should have meant, in most cases, that only those migrants whose father's father had been born in Ghana were counted as Ghanaian in origin. Thus, an elderly man whose grandfather had settled in Ghana and whose father had been born in Ghana would, strictly, be of foreign origin. It can only be supposed that enumerators must have encountered the utmost difficulty in handling the definition.

The following table relates to those of the non-Ghanaian ethnic groups for which information was made available in the census. The statistics relating to several of the ethnic groups are suspect. It would seem improbable that over a quarter of the Lobi are descendants of paternal grandfathers who settled in Ghana; probably, this high percentage reflects the fact that the Lobi (appropriately) regard themselves as permanent settlers in Ghana. The high percentage for the Pilapila only darkens the mystery regarding the origins of these peoples (see Part II). The low percentage of "Ghanaian Hausa" may be partly explained by the fact that third generation Hausa sometimes "adopt" a Ghanaian ethnic group.

THE OCCUPATIONS OF MIGRANTS IN GHANA

PERSONS OF GHANAIAN ORIGIN*

Ethnic Group	Males		Females	
	Number	Percent of Total Male Population	Number	Percent of Total Female Population
"Kyamba"	8,200	33	7,610	31
Lobi	5,310	27	5,280	30
Pilapila	3,250	26	2,960	25
Kotokoli	4,360	17	4,560	18
Fulani	2,320	14	1,890	23
"Wangara"	2,470	13	2,160	14
Mossi	8,000 †	10†	3,000†	11†
Hausa	2,930	8	2,620	11
Songhai, inc. Zabrama	770	3	460	3
"Other Nigerians"	190	1	220	2

NOTE:—No information is available for the Gurma, the Ibo, the Kru and the Yoruba.

*The statistics were obtained by deducting the "foreign origin population" from the total population of each ethnic group.

†Approximate figures: most of the "foreign origin population" of a certain residuary group were said to be Mossi.

APPENDIX IV

THE CENSUS CONCEPT OF "LOCALITY"

The census definition of "locality" was as follows:

> Apart from certain exceptions . . . each nucleated and physically distinct settlement was regarded as a separate locality for Census purposes. No particular population size is implied in the term: a locality may be a single house, a hamlet, village, town or city. An arbitrary distance of 200 yards was selected as the maximum open space, or non-built-up area, permitted between two parts of the same locality. Settlements further apart than this distance were normally regarded as separate localities. As a general principle . . . it was considered safer to err on the side of over-division than under-division since, in Census processing and analysis, it is undoubtedly easier to group together localities than to divide them (Vol. I, p. xvii).

The three exceptions mentioned were:

a) Instances where enumerators inadvertently grouped together physically separate localities under a general area name, such as Bepoase Villages, meaning "villages" in the vicinity of Bepoase. (It was stated that "fortunately, such deviations were not widespread.")

b) The Krobo and Shai *"huzas"* which were regarded as single localities, though the houses are built on a line and may be more than 200 yards apart.

c) Certain savannah districts of northern Ghana, where the population was regarded as so dispersed that "the principle of physical nucleation could not apply." In these districts "localities based upon traditional kinship groups were recorded by the enumerators."

Volume I of the Census, The *Gazetteer*, is an alphabetical and numbered list of all the localities in Ghana, showing total population and number of houses in 1960 and population in 1948, where it was thought that the localities in the two census years could be matched. In Volume II localities are grouped according to enumeration areas; an enumeration area being the area alloted to an individual enumerator. Most enumeration areas were divided into quite a small number of named localities plus a residue called "rest of enumeration area."

My purpose here is to insist that there were many more "exceptions" to the rule defining locality than the census office realized and that, in particular, the circumstances which led to the dropping of the rule in certain savannah districts of the north (exception [c]) applied equally to many other rural districts, including many in the first zone. I think that the commonsense procedure, referred to under exception (a), whereby enumerators grouped together physically separate localities under a general area name, was entirely sensible, and was possibly the usual practice. Thus on p. 41 of the official *Enumerator's Manual* the "locality" was identified with the "town or village" in which the respondent lived. From my knowledge of certain rural districts, such as South Akim Abuakwa, I would say that few of the listed localities in them are "physically separate," they are, rather, names of areas in which migrant farmers live dispersedly: some really large "localities," with populations of several hundreds, actually have no focus whatsoever and few of the houses happen to be within 200 yards of another.

In Brong-Ahafo Central, another district which attracts migrant cocoa-farmers, the omission of many large "physically distinct settlements" from the list of localities is surprising. The grouping of separate localities under a general "area name" was also common there.

It is pointed out in the introduction to census Volume II that the volume "is one of the few examples in population census publications where *small area statistics* are given for small localities and Census Enumeration Areas covering the whole country." It is unfortunate that such a truly pioneering experiment happened to be conducted in a part of the world where rural settlement patterns are apt to be such that, with the best will in the world, many enumerators were necessarily unable to follow their instructions. It is to be hoped that the published statistics by locality will not be used for the study of settlement patterns or of short-distance migration.

APPENDIX V

NOTES ON OCCUPATIONAL CLASSIFICATION IN THE CENSUS

Sampling Error

All the statistics in *Tribes in Ghana* are based on a 10 percent sample and are thus subject to sampling error (see footnote 4, p. 5).

The Census Definition of Occupation

The *kind of work* performed by the respondent *during the month preceding the census* determined his occupation. If the person "performed several different tasks (occupations) the one that was performed *most of the time* in the reference month was recorded. Only with respect to persons who did not work during the reference month but had jobs from which they were temporarily absent . . . . . was the information on occupation related to these jobs." In principle the occupation was described by the enumerator "with as much detail as possible," though there was not much room in the box on the form. The data were then processed using a less detailed classification than the international one recommended by the International Labour Office.

Family Workers

"Family workers who worked, even without remuneration, for *at least one week* during the reference month in an economic enterprise (farm, store, workshop, etc.) of another member of their household" were regarded as "occupied."

The Off-Season

The rule that those who were "temporarily absent" from their jobs should be regarded as occupied in those jobs, applied to farmers who did not work in the month preceding the census date (March 20, 1960) owing to the dry season. But "casual farm labourers" (how defined?) who did not work in the said month were regarded as unemployed. This is perhaps the explanation of the remarkably high percentages of unemployment recorded for a few ethnic groups, members of which were predominantly employed as farm labourers, notably the Kotokoli (10% unemployment) and the Pilapila (9%).

Results of the Definition

Enumerators were instructed to regard a person's occupation as that on which he spent most time during the preceding month. In a part of the world where many men, especially those in the countryside, have more than one occupation, any definition of "main occupation" must give arbitrary results. Clearly, in West African circumstances, it is quite out of the question to measure the relative importance of jobs in terms of their remunerativeness over a period (the concept of income is seldom related to fixed calendrical periods), and the acute seasonality of economic life in West Africa tends to invalidate all other types of definition based on short time-periods. The latter difficulty is of particular importance in the savannah where there is a single dry season which is long enough to give farmers time in which to pursue other types of work.

Clearly there would have been many circumstances in which rigid adherence to the census definition would have been contrary to common sense, as when a man whose main annual income was derived from cocoa-farming happened to work as a carpenter during the month ending March 20th. It is true (see *Tribes in Ghana*) that if a man did no work at all during the reference month, but had a job from which he was temporarily absent, he should have been recorded as being in that job; so if a cocoa-farmer had been wholly idle he should yet have been recorded as a cocoa-farmer. But total idleness is not nearly as common a condition as is often supposed. The probability is that many enumerators used their common sense and ignored these instructions. On the other hand, it is noteworthy that there were very few cases in which a man was recorded as having an occupation which could not conceivably be pursued in the district in which he was enumerated, which suggests that many cocoa-labourers who had returned home after the cocoa harvest had been completed, were regarded as being farmers.

Whether enumerators tended to rely to a large extent on respondents' own judgments as to their main occupation one does not know. If they did, then the importance of the most prestigeful occupations is exaggerated. A man who grows a little cocoa and much food may yet denote himself a cocoa-farmer—a serious problem considering that nearly all cocoa-farmers are also food-farmers. It is mentioned in the census reports (*Tribes in Ghana* p. civ) that there was an "inflation" of certain occupations, particularly in the professional, technical, administrative and managerial groups: while one is relieved to learn that "errors" were "corrected" as far as possible during the coding and editing process, it is a pity that in the lengthy discussion of concepts, classification and limitations of the data there is so little

APPENDIX V

reference to the kinds of decisions the editors were obliged to take—to the things that experience taught them.

Again, were remunerative occupations perhaps usually regarded as "superior" to non-remunerative ones? If so, a man who grew a little cocoa or was an occasional carpenter would be designated a cocoa-farmer or a carpenter, even when he grew sufficient food for the maintenance of a large family group.

Any definition of "main occupation" is necessarily most unsatisfactory if taken literally. On the other hand, had enumerators received more instruction on the lines on which they should use their judgment in departing from the definition, their common sense might have been less well adapted to local circumstances.

Cocoa-Farmers and *Abusa* Labourers

The most serious defect in the census, so far as the occupational statistics are concerned, is the failure in most tables (including all those in *Tribes in Ghana*,) to distinguish cocoa-farmers and *abusa* labourers separately. It is clear from such statistics relating to "caretakers" as were published in other census volumes, that the number of such persons was greatly underestimated by enumerators (see Appendix VI) and this was, presumably, the reason for the grouping of the figures in *Tribes in Ghana*, for it is anyway difficult to believe that the stated reason of "convenience of publication" could be correct, given the large numbers involved. In *Tribes in Ghana* it is stated (p. xv) that the terms *abusa* (meaning one-third) and *abunu* (one-half) express the economic relationship between the operator of the land (land-tenant) and the land-owner." But this is quite misleading. Most *abusa* men do not look after farms on behalf of absentee owners, but work alongside the farmers who employ them, from whom they do not, in any sense, rent land. It is the use of the misleading work "caretaker" (rather than *abusa*) which has been the cause, for so many decades, of so much confusion of thought.

Fortunately, however, with nearly all the 34 ethnic groups with which we are here concerned, the total recorded as "farmers or farm managers (cocoa)" is likely to consist largely of either cocoa-farmers or *abusa*, the principal exception being the Ewe; this one knows from experience in the field.

Other Cocoa-Labourers

Although for all ethnic groups taken together it is possible, using the statistics of occupation by local authority, to estimate the number of cocoa-labourers (other than *abusa*), it is unfortunately not possible to make such estimates in respect of each of the 34 ethnic groups (though some estimates are made in Part II). Consequently column (3) of Table 3 relates to all farm-labourers, whether on cocoa or food farms, exclusive of *abusa*. In *The Gold Coast Cocoa-Farmer* (1956) I classified the various types of labourer who are commonly employed on cocoa farms and enumerators would have had no difficulty in distinguishing certain of these, especially annual labourers: nor, in general, would they have found it difficult to distinguish labourers engaged primarily on cocoa farming from those engaged on growing other crops, even though most of the former do some food farming.

The Definition of "Employment"

One of the main points which I wish to emphasize is that the propensity of migrants of different ethnic groups to enter employment (proper) rather than to work on their own account, is very variable. For statistical purposes it has been necessary to make some rather arbitrary decisions on which occupations are likely to involve employment and which are likely to be pursued by "own account," or free-lance, workers—the tables relating to "employment status" in *Tribes in Ghana* do not show both occupation and ethnic group. The notes on Column (7) of Table 2 list the main occupations, in addition to farm, mining and general labourers, which are considered as involving "employment": these were, in fact, selected without reference to Table 12 in Vol. IV of the Census Report, which has since confirmed the choice. Although this latter table shows that slightly more than a half of the drivers in Ghana regard themselves as "employed" (in the public or the private sectors of the economy), it has seemed more appropriate, partly because of the great independence enjoyed by many drivers, to classify drivers generally as "own account" workers, particularly as there is a possibility that drivers who were in process of acquiring their vehicles under hire purchase agreements regarded themselves as "employed" by the hire purchase financier.

It is perhaps hardly necessary to add that the state of "employment" does not necessitate the employee being remunerated in cash: in West Africa employees are often remunerated with a share of the produce.

The census group "sales workers" is shown separately in Table 3 being there denoted as "traders": employment (proper) is rare with traders, who should be grouped with "own account" workers.

I realize, of course, that for many other purposes this concept of "employment" requires much more rigorous treatment than it has received here.

APPENDIX V

The Definition of "Own Account" Occupations

The list of occupations which are regarded as essentially "own account" is given in the notes on column (14) of Table 2. Although Table 12 of Volume IV of the Census shows that about 40 percent of "diamond diggers" (otherwise known as "African diamond winners") regarded themselves as "employees," it is thought that nearly all of them were effectively "own account" workers. This was because the economic relationship between the "tributor" (who was the actual digger) and the "licensed winner" (whose license effectively authorized him to sell diamonds won from land conceded to him) normally involved the former in effectively selling diamonds to the latter. Furthermore the tributor was usually free to dig where he liked on the land and his work was not supervised.

APPENDIX VI

ESTIMATES OF THE TOTAL NUMBERS OF COCOA-FARMERS, *ABUSA* LABOURERS AND OTHER COCOA-FARM LABOURERS

In Appendix V it is noted that the most serious defect in the census occupational statistics is the failure in most tables (including all those in *Tribes in Ghana*) to distinguish cocoa-farmers and *abusa* labourers separately. The total number of "caretakers" in cocoa-farming is given as 43,439 in Table 12 of Vol. IV of the census reports. On the basis of fieldwork in many areas of Ghana, I am convinced that the total number of *abusa* and *abunu* labourers on cocoa-farms (i.e. labourers who are rewarded with a third, or a half, of the value of the crop and whose main responsibility is that of plucking the cocoa) is far greater than 43,439; a suspicion of this possibility may have accounted for the grouping of cocoa-farmers and *abusa* labourers together in *Tribes in Ghana*. I have, therefore, made an estimate of the numbers of *abusa* labourers using the occupation figures by ethnic group. The estimates are partly based on common sense, for example, if there is no cocoa in the homeland and if members of the particular group are never recorded as being "agricultural labourers, n.e.s.," then it is probable that they migrate exclusively as farmers: they are also based on my own field experience. The chief uncertainty, so far as men are concerned, affects the Fanti, the Ashanti and the Ewe.

The census-takers also failed to distinguish agricultural labourers primarily engaged on cocoa-farms from those on food-farms. Again there are certain relevant statistics in Vol. IV Table 4 relating to the "industry," whether cocoa or food, of occupied persons—but I am sure the figures of those in cocoa are too low, perhaps partly because there was little work on cocoa-farms on the census date. I have estimated the numbers of labourers on cocoa-farms, using the statistics of the numbers of "agricultural labourers, n.e.s." in each local authority given in Table 7 of Volume IV of the census. My method of estimation is based on experience and common sense; it takes account of the general pattern of the occupational statistics in each local authority as well as the ethnic composition of the population.

According to these estimates the number of cocoa-farm labourers is about three-quarters (79%) of the number of male

THE OCCUPATIONS OF MIGRANTS IN GHANA

Occupations	Estimates (000 Males)
Cocoa farmers	222
Abusa labourers	92
Other cocoa farm labourers	83
Total cocoa labourers	175

cocoa-farmers. But some of these labourers are, of course, employed by women cocoa-farmers. The total number of women cocoa-farmers, plus *abusa*, is recorded in the census as 144,540; I estimate, on the basis of the ethnic data, that the number of women *abusa* labourers is about 4,580 (a small number, but about double the recorded number of women "cocoa caretakers" according to Table 12 of Vol. IV.) The total recorded number of other female farm labourers is 6,630; assuming, as the evidence suggests, that most of these women (say 5,000) are cocoa labourers, the total number of female cocoa-labourers (*abusa* and other) is about 10,000. Therefore, the total number of cocoa labourers (male and female) is about 185,000. The total number of cocoa-farmers (male and female) is about 364,000 (224,000 male and 140,000 female). The total number of cocoa farm labourers is, therefore conservatively estimated at about half the total number of cocoa farmers—conservatively, since it is impossible to include those migrant cocoa farm labourers who were excluded because they were in their homeland on the census date.

REFERENCES

Birmingham, W. B., *et al*.
    1966   A Study of Contemporary Ghana. The Economy of Ghana, Vol. 1. Allen and Unwin. London.

Caldwell, J. C. and C. Okonjo
    1968   The Population of Tropical Africa. Longmans. London.

Dupire, Marguerite
    1960   Planteurs autochtones et étrangers en Basse-Côte d'Ivoire orientale. Études Eburnéennes, Vol. VIII. Abidjan.

Forde, Enid R.
    1968   The Population of Ghana: A study of the spatial relationships of its sociocultural and economic characteristics. Northwestern University, Studies of Geography, No. 15.

Fortes, M.
    1945   The Dynamics of Clanship among the Tallensi. Oxford University Press.

Froelich, J-C., P. Alexandre, and R. Cornevin
    1963   Les Populations du Nord-Togo. Presses Universitaires de France.

Garlick, P. C.
    1967   The development of Kwahu business enterprise in Ghana since 1874. The Journal of African History, Vol. VIII, No. 3.

Goody, J. R.
    1956   The Social Organisation of the LoWiili. H.M.S.O. London.

    1964   The Mande and the Akan Hinterland. *In:* The Historian in Tropical Africa, edited by Vansina *et al*. Oxford University Press.

Hill, Polly
    1956   The Gold Coast Cocoa-Farmer. Oxford University Press.

    1957   Cocoa Research Series, Nos. 1 to 8. Economics Department, University of Ghana. Mimeographed.

    1963   The Migrant Cocoa Farmers of Southern Ghana. Cambridge University Press.

Lombard, M.
    1961   Les Migrations des Nord-Dahomeens au Ghana. Commission for Technical Co-operation in Africa South of the Sahara. Mimeographed.

Manoukian, Madeline
    1951   Tribes of the Northern Territories of the Gold Coast. International African Institute, Ethnographic Survey of Africa. London.

Oppong, Christine
    1967   Local Migration in Northern Ghana. Ghana Journal of Sociology, Vol. 3, No. 1.

Paques, Viviana
    1954   Les Bambara. Paris.

Rattray, R. S.
    1932   The Tribes of the Ashanti Hinterland, Vol. II. Oxford University Press.

Rouch, J.
    1956   Migration au Ghana, 1953-55. Journal de la Société des Africanistes, Vol. XXVI.

Skinner, E. P.
    1960   Labour Migration and its Relationship to Socio-Cultural Change in Mossi Society. Africa.

Tait, D.
    1961   The Konkomba of Northern Ghana. Oxford University Press.

Westerman, D., and M. A. Bryan
    1952   The Languages of West Africa. International African Institute. Oxford University Press.

Wilks, I.
    1968   The Transmission of Islamic Learning in the Western Sudan. *In:* Literacy in Traditional Society, edited by J. Goody. Cambridge University Press.